NEW FACTS ON FUTURES

Insights & Strategies for Winning in the Futures Markets

Jake BERNSTEIN

PROBUS PUBLISHING COMPANY
Chicago, Illinois
Cambridge, England

This publication is designed to provide accurate and authoritative information in regard to the subject matter covered. It is sold with the understanding that the publisher is not engaged in rendering legal, accounting or other professional service.

Authorization to photocopy items for internal or personal use, or the internal or personal use of specific clients, is granted by PROBUS PUBLISHING COMPANY, provided that the US$7.00 per page fee is paid directly to Copyright Clearance Center, 27 Congress Street, Salem MA 01970, USA. For those organizations that have been granted a photocopy license by CCC, a separate system of payment has been arranged. The fee code for users of the Transactional Reporting Service is: 1-55738-422-3/92/$0.00 + $7.00

ISBN 1-55738-422-3

Printed in the United States of America

BB

1   2   3   4   5   6   7   8   9   0

Acknowledgments

I would like to extend special thanks (not necessarily in order of importance) to the following organizations and individuals for their assistance in producing the second edition of this book:

Commodity Quote Graphics for permission to use charts from their excellent computer quotation system; R. Earl Hadady and Martin Weiss for permission to use charts from their various publications; *Intermarket Magazine* for permission to quote extensively from their Tom Baldwin and J. Peter Steidlmayer interviews; Marilyn Kinney, who runs my office, for her input which is always useful but not always immediately appreciated; and my family for their forbearance during my hours at the computer.

And a special thanks to Sally Mulroy whose valuable assistance in editing and rewriting this second edition is sincerely appreciated.

Contents

List of Tables and Figures

Prologue

An Introduction to Futures and Futures Options

For many years futures trading has been considered either too risky or too sophisticated for the average investor. Most myths are born of ignorance, and the futures myth is no exception. For all too long, futures trading was either ignored or shunned in economics texts and, as a consequence, the general public was not educated in the basics of futures. No informed choice could, therefore, be made.

Investments in securities, stocks, bonds, and even stock options, however, received considerable attention. It is generally believed that trading in stocks has more historical justification and, therefore, more value in an economic education. There are, in addition, a number of other reasons for the historically diminutive role of futures trading, few of which are valid.

So before launching into an explanation of precisely what futures trading is, it may be necessary to clear the decks of any misconceptions you may hold. First, let's examine some of the standard objections to futures trading, so that we may have a relatively clean slate upon which to write the new learning. Generally, objections to futures trading are based on either partial or distorted facts. Let's take a look at a few of these misconceptions.

1

1. **You Can Lose All You've Invested, or More, If You Trade in Futures.**

   This is true. However, the key word is *invested*. Trading futures should in no way, shape, or form be considered an investment. As a *speculation,* however, the rules of the game become distinctly different—high risk is necessary for high reward. Nevertheless, even "high risk" does not mean that the common sense rules of good trading and money management (to be taught in this book) should be ignored. It has been demonstrated clearly that a balanced investment portfolio consisting both of stocks *and* futures performs better, on average, than a portfolio consisting exclusively of stocks.

2. **Trading in Futures Is a Gamble.**

   This is another misconception. In fact, trading in futures is technically and fundamentally no different from trading in stocks. The odds of being right or wrong are essentially similar. However, due to lower margins, the odds of making money in futures are probably lower than those of making money in stocks. Ultimately, though, the possible percentage return in futures trading is considerably greater than the potential return in stocks. Futures trading is, therefore, no more of a gamble than trading in stocks. Carefully and closely following the rules of successful futures trading will help reduce the risk and gamble.

3. **Futures Trading Is for Insiders. It's a 'Rigged' Game.** (Markets are manipulated.)

   These two misconceptions go hand in hand. There is probably less inside information available in futures than there is in the stock market. The United States Department of Agriculture, the Commodity Futures Trading Commission, and the National Futures Association have imposed very stringent limits on the total number of positions a trader may hold. They monitor the brokerage industry and large trader transactions very closely. Important government information is guarded and kept strictly secret until the scheduled release date and time. In this way, the markets can function freely and with minimal effects of insider information. In fact, most markets cannot be manipulated for other than perhaps very brief periods of time since they are too complex and diverse for any one individual or group to affect prices over the long run. Unavoidably, some traders will always have an edge based on inside information, but success in the futures market is very possible without access to such information.

4. **"Trading in Futures Serves No Economic Purpose. It's a Gamble, Pure Speculation."**
This popular misconception couldn't be farther from the truth. The futures markets serve to stabilize prices. In fact, we often forget that futures markets in the U.S. were originally created to protect the farmer from volatile price moves. In today's markets this same price protection is needed—by farmers, food companies, banks, and many other large institutions, often referred to as "hedgers." The speculators provide liquidity and are often willing to take market positions when prices are fluctuating significantly due to news, weather, crop conditions, etc. This stabilizes prices by providing additional buyers and sellers to buffer extreme moves. Were it not for the speculator, prices would move more viciously, and the hedgers could not enter and exit the market as efficiently. Were it not for speculators buying and selling regardless of price levels, the markets would be subject to great volatility. Supplies would stand a good chance of being disrupted and unstable. One probable reason for the Soviet Union's demise was its lack of a delivery and exchange system for its commodities. A functional futures market would have contributed considerable stability to its economic system while also reducing producer and consumer dissatisfaction.

5. **"Futures Trading Is Only for the Short Term."**
This is also incorrect. Futures trading can be either long term, intermediate term, and/or short term depending upon the orientation of the trader. In fact, some of the most suc-

cessful futures traders, referred to as "position traders," hold
their position(s) for an intermediate- to long-term period of
time. The particular time horizon or time frame that a trader
adopts is an individual choice which does not necessarily
have to be short term to be prosperous. Many other misconceptions and misunderstandings plague futures trading, all
bred out of either partial information or ignorance. One by
one, these myths will be unveiled and corrected as your understanding of futures markets and futures trading increases. Now that a few of the major myths have been
revealed, though, we can move on to the basics of futures
trading.

EVOLUTION OF FUTURES MARKETS

Trading in futures had its origin in the development of grain trade in
the United States in the mid-1800s. The Japanese futures exchange in
silk and rice, as well as the English methods of trading iron warrants,
were precedents to U.S. futures markets.

The practice of futures trading in the United States evolved naturally from the need to protect against volatile price moves in physi-
cal grain products. Chicago took the leading role as the center of
grain futures trading. The Midwest is the heart of a rich and vast
agricultural region, and since Chicago is strategically situated as a
shipping center, it was a natural site for grain trading. The Missis-
sippi River and its tributaries were available to move grain, and later,
in conjunction with the railroads, commerce in the grain markets
flourished. The Chicago Board of Trade was organized in 1848 and
actually began trading about 1859. It was formed to meet the needs of
producers (farmers) and exporters in order to systematically manage
their risk and exposure to unknown elements, such as weather, polit-
ical events and economic uncertainty. The concept of hedging, upon
which futures markets is based, became widely used and continues
today to serve as a valuable tool for risk management.

WHAT IS HEDGING?

The concept of hedging is based upon the assumption that movement in cash and futures prices will parallel each other in movement after due allowance has been made for any seasonal or other trend in the cash market. In essence, the goal of the hedger is to lock in an approximate future price in order to eliminate his risk of exposure to interim price fluctuations.

The best way to understand hedging and the futures market is by example. I will assume that you have no understanding of the futures market.

Suppose you are a grain farmer. You grow corn. Your crop has been planted and the summer suddenly becomes hot and dry. Rain is scarce in most parts of the country, and some of the large grain-processing firms become concerned about what will happen to corn prices several months in the future as the heat and drought damage take their toll of the crop. In your area however, weather is not as bad and moisture has been sufficient. Your crops are quite good, in fact.

The grain-processing concerns such as large baking companies, animal feed manufacturers, food processors, vegetable oil producers, and other related concerns begin to buy corn from farmers and grain firms who have it in storage from previous years. Their buying is considerable due to their immense needs. Simple economics tells us that the price of corn will rise as the supply falls.

Prices begin to rise dramatically in what is called the "cash market." (This is the immediate or day-to-day market.) Another term for the cash market is the "spot market." It is so termed because it refers to transactions made on the spot, that is for immediate delivery, not for delivery at some point in the future.

Assume that you know the cost of production for your corn. In other words, you've taken into consideration your fertilizer, fuel, land, labor, and additional costs. You conclude that it costs you $1.85 to produce each bushel of corn. Your call to the local grain terminal where cash corn is bought and sold tells you that today cash corn is selling for $3.25 per bushel. Only two weeks ago it was at $3 per bushel and three months ago it was at $2.75. You know you will be producing over 50,000 bushels of corn this year and, as a consequence, the price difference between what the market was several months ago and today's price is considerable. In fact, it runs into thousands of dollars.

What are your options? You know that by the time your crop has been harvested, prices may be back down again. What could force prices back down? Many things could happen. The government could release grain from its reserves to drive prices down; foreign production could be larger than expected making the U.S. crop reduction less important; or weather could improve significantly, lessening the impact of the problem. Demand could decline and the grain companies might sell from some of the supplies they've accumulated.

Regardless of what actually happens, you've decided that you want to sell your crop at the current price. You can do either of two things:

1. You can enter into a forward contract with a grain firm. This contract is made between yourself and a grain processor or elevator. (These firms are known as "commercials.") They will quote you a price for your crop to be delivered to them at some point in the future, usually shortly after harvest. Often their price is not as high as the market's current trading level.

2. As an alternative, you could sell your crop on the futures market. The futures markets are organized exchanges or marketplaces where many individuals congregate for the purpose of buying and selling contracts in given markets for future delivery and/or for speculation. Prices there will be relatively free of manipulation by large commercial interests, which may have almost complete control over what you will be paid in your hometown area for your crop.

Provided your corn meets the proper exchange specifications, you can sell it in advance on the futures exchange. You will not get your money until the crop is delivered to the buyer, but the price you get will be locked in. Regardless of where the price goes thereafter, you will be guaranteed the price at which you sold your crop.

You could win or lose. If the cash market is higher by the time the crop is ready, you will not make as much as you might have. If the price is lower, then you are fortunate in having sold prior to the decline. Of course, you have the option of doing nothing, hoping that corn will be much higher at some point in the future. The essence of the futures market vehicle is, therefore, in its use as a tool by which the producer and end-user can hedge or protect profits. Futures are ideal hedges against rising or falling prices.

WHAT'S IN IT FOR THE PLAYERS?

Who takes the other side of the futures transaction, and why? In other words, who will buy the grain from you, why will they buy it, what will they do with it, and how will they sell it if they change their mind? Essentially, there are three categories of "players" in the futures game. They are as follows:

Producers

These individuals and/or firms actually produce or process the commodity that is being traded. Whether it be silver, gold, petroleum, corn, live cattle, lumber, sugar, or currencies, these are the people who make the goods available either by growing them, harvesting them, mining them, or lending them. They need to lock in costs. In other words, they have a product they want to sell at a determined price. They may do this in order to guarantee a profit on an actual commodity they have on hand or have produced, or they may want to lock in a price on an item in order to avoid losing more money on it if it is already declining.

Finally, they may not have the goods at all. Rather they may be protecting themselves from a possible side effect of declining or rising prices. For example, a jewelry store with considerable gold and silver jewelry on hand may fear a decline in the price of precious metals. They stand to lose money on their inventory as prices decline. Therefore, they may choose to sell futures contracts of silver and/or gold in expectation of the decline. Thus, they have profited from the futures sale.

End-Users

These are the people who will use the stuff that's sold by producers. They need to lock in the cost of their production by advance purchase of raw goods. Therefore, they will buy either on the futures market or they may make a forward contract (previously defined).

At times the end-user may become a seller as opposed to a buyer. Assume, for example, that too much has been purchased or that the final product is not selling well. In such an event, the end-user may switch to the sell side.

The producer may at times switch sides, as well. Assume that the firm does not have enough production to meet obligations to others. The producer may then become a buyer as opposed to a seller. As you can see, roles in futures trading can change.

Speculators

This is the largest group of futures traders. These people are sandwiched between the end-user and the producer, providing a market buffer. Perhaps no more than 1 to 3 percent of all futures contracts is actually completed by delivery. The balance is closed out before any actual exchange of goods occurs.

Suffice it to say that speculators are often willing to take risk in markets at times and at prices that may not be attractive to the other two groups. Speculators do this in expectation of large percentage profit returns on price fluctuations. Table 1 shows the general relationship between the three basic groups of market participants. More details will be given as your understanding of basic concepts increases.

For now I'll spare you specifics of how futures contracts work. These mechanical things will be learned later. What I want you to learn now are the concepts of futures trading. The basic issue is, of course, why trade?

TABLE 1
PLAYERS IN THE FUTURES MARKETS AND THEIR USUAL ROLES

Producers	Speculators	End-Users
Sell to lock in profits. Can buy at times. Are usually farmers, banks, mining firms, manufacturers, etc. Often called "hedgers."	Buy or sell to make a profit, but not to use the actual goods or products. Often called "traders" (among other things). Do not take delivery of the goods. Often trade for short-term swings.	Buy in order to use the product in their processing or business concern. Can be sellers at times. May not actually use the goods they buy.

WHY TRADERS TRADE

At first glance, the answer to this question is obvious. The simple fact of the matter is that traders trade, or participate in markets, in order to make profits. But there are many aspects to this simple answer. Let's look at a few of the most significant reasons for trading futures.

1. **Futures Trading Requires Relatively Small Start-Up Capital.**
   Typically, one can get started in futures trading for as little as $10,000. In some cases less capital is required. Many professionally managed trading pools require from $2,500 to $5,000 for participation. While most traders are not successful when starting with limited capital, this is one way to get your foot in the door.

   Futures options trading requires even less capital. Therefore, it is possible for the individual to begin with an even smaller amount of capital. In most other areas considerably greater capital is required. The small amount of capital can work for or against you—most often against you.

2. **Leverage Is Immense.**
The typical futures contract can be bought or sold for 1 to 3 percent of its total value. For example, a 100-troy-ounce gold contract at $400 per ounce ($40,000 cash value) can be bought for about $1,500-$2,000. The balance of the money will, of course, be due if and when the contract is completed (i.e., when you take delivery).

In the meantime, about $2,000 is controlling $40,000. In Treasury bill futures, the contract size is $1 million and the margin is about $2,500. In other words, you have immense potential using small amounts of money. This can work for you or against you. It is the goal of the futures trader to make leverage work in his or her favor.

3. **Futures Markets Make Big Moves.**
Prices fluctuate dramatically almost every day. There is considerable opportunity to win or lose daily in futures trading. Many markets will permit potential returns of 100 percent or more per day on the required margin money (i.e., money required to buy or sell a contract). This, too, can work for or against you. Where there is great opportunity, there is often great risk as well.

4. **Futures Markets Are Very Liquid.**
By this I mean that it is possible to get into or out of a market very quickly. This is not so with many stock and real estate investments. Some speculative stocks rarely trade, and real estate is often hard to dispose of quickly. With futures transactions, as with active stock transactions, one can enter and exit within minutes, or even seconds. This makes the market ideal for the speculator with limited capital.

5. **There Are Not Many Secrets to Successful Trading.**
   In some areas of investment, you need to know either the right people or the right inside information. While correct inside information can be very helpful in trading futures, success does not depend on such information. There are few secrets to successful trading. Good trading is a skill that can be learned and that can, in fact, be taught very specifically, objectively and successfully to those willing and able to learn. Virtually any individual with speculative capital, self-discipline, and the motivation to succeed has an opportunity to do so in the futures markets—but it's not easy.

6. **There Are Many Futures Vehicles.**
   In addition to the traditional buy and sell short positions, there are many vehicles in futures trading. These include options, spreads, option spreads, futures versus options positions, and combinations of the above.

WHAT ABOUT THE RISK?

You've all heard that there is considerable risk in futures trading. There's no denying this fact. The statistics are not in your favor when it comes to the futures markets. I've often heard that up to 95 percent of all traders lose their money. How does one get around these statistics?

First and foremost, education is vital. It's important to know that the trader with a small amount of capital is most apt to lose since he cannot play the game long enough to get into the highly profitable trades. The larger your starting amount, the more likely you are to be successful.

In addition, there are many time-tested principles that, if applied with consistency and discipline, will greatly improve the odds in your favor. Statistically, one can be wrong about the market over 50 percent of the time and still make money, provided losses are limited. It is the inability to keep losses small that makes most traders losers.

Furthermore, it is the behavior of taking profits quickly and losses slowly that can make the statistics work against you. The successful trader is quick to limit losses. I will come back to this point many times during the course of this book, since it is one of my goals to teach you the proper philosophy (and effective actions) of trading, in addition to the basics of the markets themselves. I am convinced that losses can be reduced by a significant degree if one learns how to limit risk, how to take losses quickly, and how to keep them small.

Losses are part of every business. In the retail or manufacturing businesses, for example, losses are comprised of such things as rent, overhead, insurance, production costs, theft, and depreciation. Not all transactions are profitable. It is, however, the bottom line that differentiates the winners from the losers.

In the final analysis, risk is something each investor and trader must evaluate in relation to his or her financial situation. It is certain that there is more inherent risk in futures trading as it is commonly practiced today. However, without risk there cannot be reward of the magnitude common in futures trading.

ADDITIONAL USES OF THE FUTURES MARKETS

This chapter has, to this point, briefly outlined preliminary concepts and applications of futures trading. Naturally, as a vehicle for speculating, hedging, or spreading risk, futures trading has significant importance. As a vehicle for stabilizing costs to producers and end-users, futures trading is a vital tool.

On a more pervasive level, however, an understanding of futures trading can prove very valuable to the investor not interested in actually trading futures. This book gives considerable attention to the hypothesis that a knowledge of futures price trends and futures market behavior can assist one in understanding economic trends as well as in forecasting the short-term to intermediate-term direction of prices. There may also be long-range implications for investors.

CONCLUSIONS

Futures trading is a technique whereby one can buy and/or sell a variety of raw and processed commodity items, including financial instruments and stock indices, for anticipated delivery at some point in the future. There are three major categories of participants in the futures markets, each with their own expectations, goals, and market methods. Futures trading allows producers and end-users to lock in costs of production, improving economic stability as well as the stability of their particular business. Speculators, by far the largest category of traders, have no interest in making or taking delivery. Rather, their interest is in playing market swings for dollar profits.

There are many common objections to futures trading. Some have merit; others are not well-founded.

There are specific methods, systems, and procedures used in futures trading designed to reduce its inherent risk, a majority of which have been time-tested. Futures trading involves considerable risk. However, this risk can be greatly reduced by consistent application of various principles. Futures trading can be an excellent vehicle for immense profit, or it can be a dangerous tool for financial ruin. Those who win often attribute their success to an attitude which reflects self-discipline, courage, consistency, persistence, specific trading techniques, and a willingness to learn from mistakes.

Part 1

Getting Started: Myths and Realities of the Futures Markets

Chapter

1

Dealing with Basic Issues First

It sometimes seems that the older we get, the more complex our lives become. But by complicating simple issues we do ourselves a disservice. The stock and futures markets are, for example, relatively easy to understand as long as we do not allow ourselves to become intimidated.

My first exposure to the markets was in an eighth-grade social studies class. The instructor thought it would further our education in economics and the "American Way" if we were to hypothetically invest a thousand dollars in several stocks we selected from the evening newspaper listings. "Why should we do this?" asked one of the students. "To make our capital grow," replied the teacher. He elaborated on our assignment by offering the following concise explanation of how the American capitalist system works (which I have paraphrased).

Our system of economics functions on the basis of supply and demand. Supply and demand make prices go up and down. In order to meet demand, individuals form associations or businesses to supply the goods, services, or commodities that the public wishes to consume. However, in order to do this they require capital.

There are many ways in which they can raise the required capital. One of the most common is the issuance of stock. Shares of stock are issued to buyers who will, in effect, lend their money to the company which will, in turn, produce the products. The shareholders' reward for lending money to the corporation will be participation in the profits.

Of course, there is no guarantee profits will be made, and so the purchase of stock is a gesture of good faith and expectation based on the buyer's perception of the company's ability to make good on its business ventures. In addition, if the company does exceptionally well, the demand for its stock will grow and the shareholder can make money in two ways. First, money can be made on a share of profits distributed by the company. Second, money can be made when the stock price goes up in response to demand from individuals wanting to purchase a part (or shares) of that company.

This definition was simple enough and certainly satisfied everyone of us in class. We felt as if the answer to making money in the stock market was rather simple. Referring to this often shared notion about the stock market, Will Rogers once said something like, "Making money in the stock market is simple. Just find stocks that are going to go up and buy them." The simple-minded solution offered by our teacher was easily accepted by us in those days and was sufficient for many years to come. However, with the experience I've gained over time, I find this issue, once elementary, has now become immensely complex.

Similarly, there are many other basic issues that appear simple on the surface but become highly complex when examined in detail. The balance of this chapter deals with some of these issues, not necessarily in order of importance but in considerable detail. These are all issues that each current or prospective speculator must evaluate. There is always a great temptation for students to glide over the introductory portion of a book in order to get on with the real meat of the subject. This book is all "real meat." In fact, I would venture to say that the major substance is contained in the first few chapters as opposed to the last few. So, if you are going to skim, don't skim this chapter!

Take your time. Think each issue through thoroughly and, above all, be honest with yourself. Don't take any of these issues lightly, even though you may be familiar with all of them. The facts of futures trading will only be helpful to you if you have a solid background against which to apply these concepts.

GRIST FOR THE MILL

The world of well-dressed brokers, white-collar executives, and the man in the pinstripe suit who "listens while his broker talks," is not the real world of trading. There is a story behind every trade, and a trade behind every story. More often than not, it is not a very pleasant one.

The tale is not based upon the simple act of picking up a telephone and calling in an order. The true story behind the crisp numbers crossing the ticker tape or flashing on your computer screen is one of competition, psychology, strategy, skill, victory, and defeat. A good majority of traders have been and will continue to be losers. Accept this fact now, or you too will be nothing but grist for the mill.

Contrary to most beliefs, success in the futures markets is not based on acquiring more information. If you believe success is achieved by simply acquiring more information, then it is time to re-evaluate your thinking process. In order to avoid the unfortunate fate of most speculators, you will need to think and act in a fashion contrary to most traders. You will need to learn to think for yourself. You will use the available market tools, but you will reach different conclusions and you will take different actions. In order to do this you will need to:

1. Examine your objectives and recognize the problems (if any).

2. Formulate your plan of action and solve the problems.

3. Make a commitment.

4. Select the vehicle you will use to transport you to your goals.

5. Put your plans into action with consistency and discipline.

Knowledge alone is not the key to effective action. You can do endless hours of research, but without taking action in the market, the knowledge will not help you to produce results.

In order to make money in futures trading, you will have to find a way to take money legally from other traders before they take it from you. In futures trading the cold hard facts are simply these: For every winner there is a loser; for every dollar made, there is a dollar lost; you can profit only at the expense of someone else's loss. If you don't make others the grist for your mill, you will become the grist for theirs.

OBJECTIVES

To seek perfection in the futures market is not only impractical, but impossible. None of us, including this writer, will ever attain the level of perfection we seek in futures trading. The first lesson in establishing objectives is to keep your goals realistic. There are ways to measure our standard of expectations while keeping our goals in perspective. In reality, we may secretly wish and hope to surpass these standards by a significant amount, but we should not overestimate our abilities by placing our expectations beyond the realm of the real futures world.

What, then, is realistic? Let's examine the facts in terms of performance and profits. First let's take a look at the performance of professionally managed funds over an extended period of time.

Managed Account Reports[1] states that, of the professionally managed commodity funds now in operation, one of the largest cumulative percentage profits since inception amounted to 30.4 percent. This covered a period of six years. Note that since commodity-managed funds began reporting their results, approximately 14.5 percent of them have been liquidated at losses of 50 percent or greater.

---

1   Lee Rose. *Managed Accounts Reports*. 5513 Twin Knolls Road, Suite 213, Columbia, Maryland, 21045.

The best overall performance of such programs is in the area of 19.1 to 30.4 percent of starting equity. Remember, this does not take into consideration the funds that have been closed out at 50 percent losses or more.[2]

In order to have realistic expectations, we can use the foregoing parameters of performance as our guidelines. Taking an average, you can see that 19–31 percent profit per year is a realistic expectation. Don't be dismayed—19–31 percent compounded at an annual rate works out to be a very high figure.

CAN YOU MAKE THE COMMITMENT?

Consider the results I have just discussed. These results were obtained by full-time professionals in the commodity business. Their work required a major commitment of time and effort. Although it is probably true that there is not a one-to-one relationship between profits and efforts extended in the futures markets, it is true that considerable effort is necessary in order to achieve reasonably good results. You must assess your efforts and goals realistically in terms of the time commitment you can make.

People, generally, are long on ambition but short on effort. But even effort, in and of itself, does not guarantee profitable trading. Effort must be directed at a particular goal. It must be guided through proper steps. Effort must be aimed in the right direction. It must be self-correcting. Patience and a willingness to learn from mistakes is needed. All of this takes time! Perhaps the greatest favor you can do for yourself is to be realistic in terms of time. This leads to the next issue.

HOW WILL YOU ACHIEVE YOUR GOAL?

The goal of profits in futures trading can be achieved through many ways—long-term trading, short-term trading, speculating on an in-

---

2   Figures through end of 1985.

traday basis, spreading, options trading, option spreads, floor trading, as a broker, or by a combination of these strategies. In addition,
there are many vehicles which can lead you toward, or away from,
your goals. You must make some important decisions as to how you
will achieve your goals. Some of these decisions can be made based
on your present knowledge. Others, however, cannot be made until
you have a broader understanding of the field. I would suggest that
even if you feel you already know the answers to these issues, you
come back and reread this section after you have finished reading the
entire book. In future chapters, I will revive some of these pressing
issues, providing you with some suggestions as to their resolution.

THE VEHICLE

Many vehicles can take you to your goal. Some will lead you in the
right direction, whereas others will take you in the wrong direction.
These vehicles are the systems and methods of futures trading.

I can't tell you which system is best for you. All I can do is to
acquaint you with the various methods and with guidelines for deciding which techniques are best for you. The performance of trading
systems is not static. Systems go through good times as well as bad.
Traders go through good times as well as bad. Traders and systems
interact in a complex combination.

I can't give you the ultimate answers, but I can acquaint you
with the tools. I can give you the knowledge to help you make your
own decisions based upon the facts. As you read the remainder of
this book, keep your mind tuned to the issues I have just raised,
looking for answers as you go. Assuming that you have already had
some experience in this area, you will recognize the answers more
easily.

THE FUEL

In your travels you will need a goal, a vehicle, and fuel. We have
already discussed the vehicle and the goal. Now we must look at the
fuel.

The energy that drives the wheel of successful speculation is good old-fashioned money. To make it, you have to have it, and to multiply it you have to use it wisely. You know that risk is immense and that the odds are stacked against you. Your chances of making it in the competitive world of futures trading are probably five or ten in 100, but they are reduced to zero by starting with nothing. Successful speculation is not a get-rich-quick scheme, a no-money-down real estate venture, or a 15-million-to-one odds lottery ticket. The facts of futures trading dictate very clearly that the more you start with, the greater your chance of success, and the less you start with, the greater your chance of failure.

"How much is enough?" you ask. I can give you some guidelines. Based on 1986 conditions in the futures market, the beginner should have sufficient capital to meet liberal marginal requirements on at least five contracts in the futures market. If we assume, for example, that the average margin on a futures contract is $2,500, then we are looking at approximately $12,500 in speculative capital. I don't think it is realistic for you to expect success if you begin with less.

Don't be fooled! Some individuals will tell you that you need virtually nothing in the way of starting capital, whereas others will tell you you need much, much more. I won't argue the fact that the more you have to start with the better your odds of success; however, there is a limit on the downside. Certainly you must consider the fact that you don't want to risk everything. When someone asks me how much they should risk in futures trading, I answer the question with a question. I ask, "How much can you afford to lose?" One answer might be $10,000. "Take this slip of paper on which I have written $10,000," I respond. "Rip it into shreds. Flush it down the toilet. How do you feel?"

This small test represents a little experiment that may help you determine how much you can afford to lose in the futures market without too serious an emotional reaction to the consequences. Financially, the answer is different. How much can you afford to lose from this standpoint? I would suggest that as a rule of thumb, you risk not more than 25 percent of your total liquid risk capital!

DON'T BORROW YOUR STARTING CAPITAL

Let me caution you against a practice I have witnessed on a number of occasions during my years in the futures market. It has become more and more common for individuals to borrow money in order to speculate in futures. Specifically, second mortgages or home equity loans are often used for this purpose. I recommend you do not consider this foolish behavior. There is no sound judgment in such behavior and the results of such actions can be disastrous. The individual not only places him or herself at financial risk, but jeopardizes his or her trading by using funds that should not and cannot be placed at risk. Certainly it takes no great insight to see that the trading decisions of the speculator will be based on fear and this will seriously affect his or her judgment.

Another pitfall to avoid is the following mental trap: "I'll put more money into my account than I intend to lose, but the rest will draw interest and, of course, I will watch the money closely." As I explained, this is a rationalization based on unrealistic thinking. Even with the best intentions, when "extra" money is in the account, chances are it will be used for trading. Put into your account only what you can afford to lose in its entirety.

Don't be fooled by the lure of interest rate earnings on the unused funds, especially low-risk trading programs, fail-safe programs, "no risk" option strategies, minimal risk spreading programs, and a host of other seemingly simple "minimal risk" programs. I've seen them come and I've seen them go. There are some big winners, but there are many, many more big losers. Do not accept the claims of any trading system, your own or that of someone else, as the basis for deciding how much of your money you will place at risk.

REACH YOUR GOAL BY STAGES

The most fruitful and consistent means to achieve a goal is through stages or steps. Unfortunately, or perhaps fortunately, our dimension in time and space does not permit thoughts to become actions instantaneously and, therefore, goals must be attained slowly. Whether you decide to trade for the short, intermediate, or long term, it is advisable that you regularly withdraw profits from your account once you have reached a certain level of successful performance. Generally, I recommend 10 to 25 percent of profits be removed from every winning trade of your account. This need not be done on a trade-by-trade basis. You can do it weekly or perhaps bi-monthly, but remember to do it!

More speculators would be successful if they approached futures trading as though it were a business. After a period of learning and initial cost, a business that reaches the point of profitable operation will generate income for its operator(s). The profits are then taken and employed in some other fashion not directly connected with the business itself. Some of the other profits are turned back into the business in order to expand its base.

It is the same with futures trading. On occasion, speculators have achieved tremendous initial growth in their accounts. Lured by greed and the promise of even greater profits, they have plowed every penny, if not more, back into the market, only to lose it all. When all is said and done, they have nothing to show for their great efforts.

This is why you must formulate and institute a specific program for systematically removing a percentage of your profits from your trading account. This rule is applicable whether you are speculating for the long term, short term, or an intermediate time frame.

OTHER IMPORTANT ISSUES

In addition to the points just raised, a number of important issues warrant attention from all aspiring futures traders, regardless of their eventual orientation, system, or trading methodology. I will review some of these briefly at this time, covering them in greater detail as the occasions present themselves in future chapters.

1. **Trade Alone or with a Partner?**
   There are pros and cons to each alternative. If you trade alone, there will be no one to help you with your work (unless you hire employees) and there will be no one who can trade for you in your absence. Furthermore, there will be no one with whom you can discuss various markets, indicators, techniques, and trades. To those individuals who need this

type of assistance, a partner or well-trained assistant might be desirable. However, before you make such a decision consider the potential negatives of having a partner.

    a.   **Too Many Cooks Spoil the Pie.** Futures trading is a "loner's game." Sometimes a partner or partners will get in your way. You may be influenced to avoid some trades you should have made and to make some trades you should have avoided.

    b.   **Who's Responsible?** In developing your trading, it is always good to know that you alone have the responsibility for profits and losses. If you have a partner or partners, it may be difficult to know who is responsible for each decision. Lacking such knowledge will slow the learning process and may, in fact, stall it entirely.

    c.   **Sharing the Profits.** Do you really want to share your profits with partners? Granted, they may also share in your losses, but since you may end up with more losses if you have partners, the benefits may prove nil.

    d.   **Do You Want to Share Your Research?** Many of us consider our research proprietary. We work long, hard hours to develop trading systems and methods and we may not want to share these with a partner regardless of what he or she may bring into the relationship.

    e.   **Slower Decision Time.** As you know, decisions in the futures markets must be made quickly. Many times the presence of a trading partner may slow down the decision-making process and, hence, severely limit the speed with which you can execute orders. This, as you can well imagine, can frequently have negative results.

2. **Trade for the Short Term, Long Term, or Intermediate Term**
I could write several books just addressing this subject. There are so many variables to consider, not the least important of which are your personality and temperament.

Here are just a few of the factors you should consider in making this decision.

a.   **Trading System.** Some trading systems are more ideally suited to short-term trading, while others are better suited to long-term trading.

b.   **Time Availability.** Only you know how much time you have available. To trade for the short term or intraday you will need to make a major time commitment. If you have another job and you can't make this commitment, don't even try! Be realistic and determine what you can do with the time you have available. This may automatically make your decision for you.

c.   **Commissions.** Are you paying sufficiently low commissions to permit short-term trading with a positive bottom line?

d.   **Personality.** Can you take the pressure of short-term trading? Are you more in tune with long-term trading, its less demanding pace and the patience required?

e.   **Health.** Believe it or not, health is a consideration. If your health is at stake, then by all means don't push your luck. Trade with that period of time in mind which will best be suited to any health concerns. Answering this question honestly will help make many decisions for you without considering any of the other aspects.

f.   **Data.** Many individuals are under the false impression that they can day-trade the market without a steady source of tick-by-tick data. Don't fool yourself! To day-trade you need up-to-date, tick-by-tick, accurate, and reliable data. If you can't afford it, if you don't know how to use it, then don't kid yourself. Day-trading is not for you. In addition to the above, there are other factors which are specific to your individual situation that must be considered before a final decision is made about the type of trading you wish to do. This is an important decision. Do not take it lightly.

3. **Fundamental or Technical**
    Another important decision which ideally should be made prior to the start of your trading is whether your approach will focus primarily on trading signals from technical indicators or from trading ideas based upon fundamentals. I distinguish here between ideas and signals because they are two distinctly different types of approaches generated by two distinctly different understandings of the futures markets.

    Later on I will provide a very thorough discussion of the two approaches, outlining their strengths, assets, liabilities, differences, and methods of implementation. For now, suffice it to say that a decision will need to be made, preferably sooner than later, about the approach you wish to employ in your trading. Some individuals may seek to implement a hybrid approach, incorporating what they feel are the best aspects of each technique. I also will discuss the merits of this approach, or the lack thereof.

4. **How Much Risk Do You Want to Take on Each Trade?**
    A significant question, one that is perhaps best answered prior to the start of trading is, "How much do you want to risk on each trade?" Many factors enter into this decision, and there are many different opinions regarding the best answer.

    On opposite ends of the continuum, we find the two most extreme approaches. Those who belong to the "money management school" will tell you that the best approach to take is a per-trade risk based strictly on money management. In other words, you decide ahead the maximum risk you want to take, in dollars. When a trade goes against you by the predetermined amount, you close it out. On the other end of the spectrum is the "systems approach." Proponents of this approach claim that each trade is unique. Every trade has specific levels of support and resistance and, therefore, it is not possible to determine *a priori* a rule for dollar risk. My approach to this aspect of futures trading is essentially similar to my approach in other areas. I prefer not to be in the middle of the road. Rather, I would align myself with either of the extremes.

As you continue to read this book, you will understand more clearly why my preference is usually to be found on one end of the spectrum or the other, but rarely in the middle. It's been said that you can walk on the left side of the road or the right side of the road, but if you walk in the middle of the road you will get squashed.

There are merits to each approach and there is no right or wrong answer to the question. There is, however, an answer that is *your* answer. My job is to help you find it. Hopefully, by the time you have finished this book, you will have found the answer falling naturally into place. For the time being, however, I will tell you that each approach has its strong and weak points and you can be successful by following either of the extremes.

SELECTING A BROKER

This topic is so important that I have devoted a full chapter to it. You needn't make the decision now. Many of you may, in fact, already have a broker (or brokers).

A broker can help you or hurt you. I do not contend that brokers intentionally hurt customers. Certainly this would not be in their best interest. I am saying, however, that on various levels, the relationship between broker and client is extremely important, and that insufficient attention has been given to this variable. Virtually no book I've read on successful methods of speculation places sufficient emphasis on this variable and its potentially positive/negative implications. When you are done reading this book, your ideas about the broker/client relationship likely will have changed significantly.

The foregoing issues are ones you should consider prior to serious speculation in the futures markets. There will be many other important issues raised by this book, but the ones outlined in this chapter should develop within your unconscious mind while you read the chapters that follow.

I want to stress that some of the material discussed in the balance of this book will not be new to you. In fact, I am certain that the issues I have discussed in this chapter are ones with which you are essentially familiar right now. Don't let the oldness of the ideas stand in the way of your acquiring new and valuable understandings of old information. If you consider the fact that most market analysts and speculators have the same information at their disposal, but that some use it with considerably more success than others, you will understand that the difference between losers and winners is not necessarily that winners have better tools, but rather that they use their tools better. How to use tools for maximum results is what this book will attempt to teach you.

SUMMARY

It was explained that success in the futures markets can come only at the expense of other traders' failures. The factors affecting success were identified and discussed. Guidelines were set out for realistic objectives in light of performance, and committed effort was stressed. Amount and sources of starting capital needed were discussed, along with a procedure for withdrawing proceeds from profitable trades. The benefits and drawbacks of trading with a partner were covered. Long-term, short-term, and intermediate-term time orientations were considered, as were preferences for technical or fundamental trading systems and the choice among levels of risk. The broker-client relationship was discussed briefly.

Chapter

2

Trading Approaches: Fundamental Versus Technical Analysis

Let's begin by exploring a basic controversy of futures trading. Since this book will challenge many concepts and beliefs revered by a majority of speculators, let's not waste any time before the iconoclasm begins. Let's look at what I call the "good, the bad, and the ugly"— fundamentals, technicals, and the peculiar offspring of their marriage that one might, for public relations purposes, term "eclectics."

We will take a critical overview of the two major approaches, then examine their hybrid in order to see which, if any, might be the most desirable approach. Please understand that what is being expressed herein are the opinions of one speculator. They may be right; they may be wrong. They may ultimately be proven valid or invalid, but they are designed to stimulate thought, and in so doing, to promote positive change. The markets function on the basis of opinion.

We all know that opinions are plentiful. However, opinions based on considerable experience should not be dismissed lightly.

FUNDAMENTAL ANALYSIS

What in heaven's name is a fundamental? I have often asked myself this question. It seems that everything is fundamental. Do we mean fundamental as opposed to trivial or fundamental in the sense of basic or fundamental in the sense of building block? Let's look at a recent definition of the term as found in the *Handbook of Futures Markets*.[1] Note also some of the points raised by the analysis.

The fundamentalist uses historical economic information to establish a supply-and-demand price curve. He or she then relates estimates of this year's supply-and-demand balance to the historical price to decide if the current price is too high, too low, or just right. To arrive at an estimate of this year's supply, the fundamentalist will examine reports of the number of acres planted with a particular crop. The fundamentalist also will look at the sales of fertilizer, and the sales and cost of diesel fuel for farm equipment in addition to past weather data and predicted weather patterns for both the near- and longer-term periods of the crop's growing season. Information must be taken into account about the productivity of new seeds or strains developed for the crop being considered, or for competing crops. The fundamentalist must be aware of the government stockpiles as well as those stockpiled on-farm (visible supply). Government price-support levels and the strength of the dollar will be considered, as they affect exports. The analyst will weigh the cost of interest paid on borrowed money, the impact of competition from substitutes or new products, and will be alert to changes in eating patterns and per capita income affecting demand. This list would have to be extended significantly to include all the primary determinants of price, and yet the accuracy of the current price evaluation would depend on the accuracy of the estimates and the weighting of factors. Do not think, though, that because of the complexity of the

---

1   P.J. Kaufman (Wiley: New York, 1985), 16.5.

information involved, no fundamental method, as we have defined it, can be possible.

There are econometric formulas which, using computers, can reduce this mass of data to specific values, with respect to the current price and provide adequate information for trading purposes.

The difficulty with the fundamental approach for most speculators is that vast amounts of time and money can be consumed to obtain the past and present data, and to work it into reliable formulations. To continue to update this data each day would then be the task of a full-time staff. (Time-sharing computer services which provide this information are equally expensive.) The individual trader who wishes to use the fundamental approach is in direct competition with the largest producers and processors in the world, with their relatively unlimited resources of information and analysis. In such a competition, the outcome is not often a surprise.

Fundamentals, then, are the economic realities that ultimately affect price. Fundamentalists, then, are those who somehow formulate a trading plan or trading approach on the basis of fundamentals. In other words, they take the basics of supply/demand, and determine whether prices should increase or decrease. On the basis of these expectations, they make buy and sell decisions.

Fundamental analysis has its roots in economics, and there are many economic theories. Similarly, there are many different approaches to fundamental analysis. The common element of all approaches to fundamental analysis is that they study the purported causes of price increases and price decreases in the hope that they will be able to ascertain changes prior to their occurrences. Their success rests upon the availability of accurate assessments of the variables they analyze, as well as the availability of variables that may not be known to other fundamental analysts.

The surplus of statistics available to the fundamentalist at any given point in time can be overwhelming. The fundamentalist must be selective and be prepared to evaluate a massive amount of data.

There is no one typical fundamentalist. We won't find a cage in the zoo labelled, "Analyticus Fundamentalis." Rather, there are many different types of fundamentalists, who evaluate different types of data at different times. There are those who, by virtue of their skill and their expertise, can provide accurate forecasts, and there are those who, working with the same tools, make worthless forecasts.

SHORTCOMINGS OF FUNDAMENTAL ANALYSIS

The popularity of computer technology has, unfortunately, overshadowed the excellent work being done by many individual researchers in the area of fundamental analysis. The tendency of modern society to look for quick and easy solutions to problems has been partially responsible for the shift away from public implementation of fundamental analysis. On the other hand, the contemporary trend toward simpler solutions has, in part, been stimulated by the difficulty and complexity of fundamental analysis.

The average individual will have very limited success in understanding, analyzing, and implementing massive amounts of fundamental statistics. Even if all relevant statistics were available, the average individual would have difficulty interpreting their meaning as it relates to the important issue of futures trading, which is timing. Some of the difficulties with fundamental analysis can be summarized as follows:

1. Not all fundamentals can be known at any given time.

2. The importance of different fundamentals varies at different times. It is difficult to know which fundamentals are most significant at which time.

3. The average speculator may have difficulty gathering and interpreting the wealth of information that is available for every market.

4. Fundamental analysis often fails to answer the important question that faces most speculators—the question of timing.

5. Most fundamental statistics are available after the fact. By the time they are gathered by various government agencies or reporting services throughout the world, they are often

old information and do not necessarily reflect the immediate situation.

6. Fundamentals can be significantly altered by abrupt changes such as weather, politics, international events, and some technical factors. It may take time for these items to be reflected in the fundamental statistics.

7. The amount of effort required in gathering, updating, and interpreting fundamental data may not, in the long run, yield efficient results.

8. Most fundamental analysis does not provide alternatives based on price action, but rather it provides alternatives based on changes in underlying conditions. These changes may be so slow that no visible or perceptible alterations in bullish or bearish stance can be justified when, in fact, a major change in trend may have begun.

Yet, in spite of these shortcomings, fundamental analysis still has its place in the commodity world. Ultimately, the price of every commodity is a function of fundamentals. Unfortunately, fundamental analysis has been the whipping boy of market technicians for many years now. Whether justified or not, this has led to an understatement of its importance.

Rest assured that the fundamentals are very important and that their implementation can yield significant results over the long term. I maintain that fundamental analysis has its place for the intermediate- and long-term trader. However, for the short-term speculator I would suggest that fundamentals are not likely to yield the results you seek. The individual who is willing to establish a major position, stick with the position, give it plenty of leeway, and possibly add to the position on a scale-in basis, can do very well. This is the proper place for the fundamentalist.

Typically, individuals employed to provide price forecasts, hedging patterns, purchasing programs, and planning programs for commercial end-users or suppliers are especially good at understanding and implementing fundamentals. These individuals are not

primarily concerned with timing. Frequently they can ride through
virtually any storm. The speculator however, cannot use the same
approach since his or her capital, time, patience, and tolerance are
limited by the constraint of available resources.

APPLYING FUNDAMENTALS

Fundamental analysis is not the anathema so many contemporary
traders consider it to be. Fundamentals form the basis of the economic equation. Too often they will be proven correct after the fact
with virtually 100 percent accuracy. Even such unexpected events as
changes in weather ultimately will be reflected in the fundamental
statistics, forecasting price level and direction, but response time can
be slow.

The interpretation of fundamentals is both a science and an art
which most speculators and average futures traders will have difficulty implementing. Experience and knowledge are especially important in the analysis and implementation of fundamentals. They
cannot be acquired as quickly as can the experience in the area of
technical analysis.

If you are still interested in the application of fundamentals, I
suggest that you take the following advice to heart:

1. Study economics thoroughly. Acquaint yourself with the
    various micro and macro economic theories, particularly as
    they apply to production and consumption.

2. Acquire a thorough knowledge of the production, consump-
    tion, critical factors, and implementation of the various com-
    modities you wish to trade.

3. Attempt to specialize, but do not exclude all other markets
    from your perspective. There are so many factors to consider
    that you cannot keep abreast of many markets and economic
    trends. You cannot be in touch with all market factors and
    all markets at one time, even with the aid of a computer.
    Therefore, you ought to specialize in one or two groups of
    markets (i.e., meats, grains, metals, currencies).

4. Plan to spend several years learning the application of fundamentals. This is a highly complex field, one which is not mastered easily. Once mastered, however, the benefits can be substantial for the intermediate and long-term trader (investor).

TECHNICAL SYSTEMS

With the exception of the complete novice to futures trading, virtually everyone is familiar with one or several aspects of technical analysis. Technical analysis is loosely defined as a study of futures trading data and its derivatives with the goal of forecasting price and/or determining specific market timing. In plain old English, this means that the technical analyst studies such things as price, volume, open interest, and chart patterns, as well as their interrelations, permutations, and combinations. The goal of most technical analysis is not necessarily prediction; it is the determination of specific entry and exit levels, and/or specific price objectives for each signal. But prediction is not a requirement. Entry and exit signals alone are quite sufficient.

The roots of technical analysis run deep under the history of futures trading. It is difficult to say with certainty who the first individual or group to employ technical analysis might have been. I am certain, however, that traces of technical analysis can probably be found as far back as ancient civilizations. Since technical analysis prides itself on having a quasi-scientific basis, you can understand how the continued exponential growth of scientific methodology has spilled over into the area of technical analysis (as well as fundamental analysis). As a consequence, there are literally hundreds of systems, methods, techniques, and trading approaches based on technical concepts.

Technical analysis certainly has its place in the world of futures trading, but as you might have guessed it certainly has its limitations as well. It is my conclusion that technical analysis is more suitable for short-term trading than for long-term trading. Although there are certain technical methods which may be applied to long-term charts, the intricacies of technical analysis do not easily lend themselves to such things as contract changes (i.e., length of contract life) in the futures market.

Specifically, long-term technical analysis must employ long-term data. The only continuous long-term data available to futures analysts is cash market data. Futures data starts and stops with contract expirations and contract inceptions. The variability of prices from one contract to another as a function of such things as carrying charges, storage charges, and interest rates creates a gap that must be filled either by creation of artificial data or by some other statistical manipulation that is not necessarily representative of true underlying conditions. Due to this fact, there have been a number of different approaches to technical analysis on weekly and monthly charts, resulting in some disagreement among followers of the various techniques. Some of the criticisms of technical analysis are:

1. Pure technical analysis ignores all extraneous inputs such as news, fundamentals, weather, etc. This is seen as a detriment by some, since these factors can and do significantly affect prices.

2. Technical analysis is a form of tunnel vision, since it accepts input from no other method or technique when employed in its ideal form.

3. Technical analysis is so widely used, particularly by computer-generated trading programs, that many systems act in unison, thereby affecting prices in a fashion that is not representative of the true price structures.

4. Technical analysis cannot allow for good forecasting or determination of price objectives since it does not account for underlying economic conditions.

5. Technical analysis is not a valid scientific approach since most methods study prices based upon price related data. In a sense, one is attempting to predict the outcome of a dependent variable based upon the history of the dependent variable. If the variable is indeed dependent upon circumstances

external to it, then it is a fallacy to attempt such predictions without knowing the external circumstances.

6. Technical analysis is a self-fulfilling prophecy and clearly typifies the greater fool theory.[2] In the end, it is the individual who is stuck with the hot potato who pays the price of being the greatest fool.

These, then, are some of the objections to technical analysis. On the positive side, however, technical analysis attains its strength from the fact that it is a form of disciplined and essentially mechanical application of trading rules. In its ideal form, technical analysis leaves little or no room for interpretations of trading signals. In this way, it permits discipline to regulate trading. Naturally, these are ideal concepts and their application is most certainly dependent upon the individual. Some advantages of the purely technical approach are:

1. **Objectivity:** The technical approach, in ideal form, is objective and specific. It is akin to scientific methodology.

2. **Specificity:** The technical approach looks for specific indications from the data and then acts upon them. Hence, there should be little or no room for interpretation in a purely technical method.

3. **Mechanical:** Many technical analysts claim their approach is totally mechanical. In other words, no thought must go into the buying/selling decisions. The system makes all the judgments and the trader follows them mechanically (when the system is implemented in its ideal form).

4. **Testable:** All results and indicators can be tested and verified historically. This makes the approach more scientific and lends credence to its use and value.

---

2   The belief that if one buys a particular stock, commodity, or piece of property, one need only wait for someone else who is a greater fool to sell it to.

5. **Cross-User Reliability:** The technical approach should yield similar results regardless of who is using the system, provided their rules are the same. However, this is not the case with many technical approaches, since they leave a certain amount of room for interpretation.

6. **Ease of Application:** By virtue of the above, technical systems are claimed to be easier to implement than are fundamentally based systems.

7. **Computer Application:** Recently, the advent of lower-priced personal computer systems has made technical systems even less difficult to test and employ. Most truly mechanical systems can be programmed into computers, which will generate all buy and sell signals accurately. In some cases computers can even be programmed to send the signals to a broker for execution.

There is much to be said in favor of technical analysis. However, with the growing ability of computer systems to work with complex econometric models, I expect to see fundamentally based computer models reach a growing level of impact on futures trading during the 1990s and beyond. The result could very well be a hybrid approach that yields better performance than each method alone. This, however, is not yet the case. Whether technical, fundamental, or techno-fundamental, the ultimate action taken by the speculator will determine the success or failure of any trading system, regardless of how promising computer tests of the system may be.

WHAT'S BEST FOR YOU

It is my observation that individuals who adhere strictly to one approach or another can do well in the marketplace. However, individuals who are constantly shifting from one technical approach to another, from one fundamental approach to another, or from an essentially fundamental point of view to a technical point of view will probably not do well. This is because they do not allow sufficient time for their trading approach to reach fruition.

The answer to the question, "What's best for you?" is not a simple one. After years of analysis and study, I can tell you that virtually any systematic approach to futures trading can be successful, provided that it contains three essential elements:

1. **Specific Entry and Exit Indicators.** By this I mean that rules for entering and exiting trades must be as specific and mechanical as possible. Interpretation and deliberations about the validity of a given indicator must be kept to an absolute minimum. There also should be reliability between different users of the method. In other words, two individuals using the same approach on the same market at different locations and without collaboration should ideally reach the same conclusion.

2. **Money Management.** In order for a system to be successful, it must have an automatic way to limit losses. There should be a maximum permissible dollar loss or a specific level beyond which losses should not go on, regardless of what the system says.

3. **Flexibility.** The system must be sufficiently flexible to trade both sides of the market, long and short. Furthermore, the system should do well in all types of markets, trending and trendless (though this is a lot to ask).

SUCCESS AT THE EXTREMES

Provided these essential elements are present, and provided the method of selection has a slightly greater probability than chance, the end result should be profitable. Many systems are capable of generating trading signals that are profitable more than 50 percent of the time. Many approaches, both technical and fundamental, could have even better performance by applying various trend filters.

For now, suffice it to say that the technical approach to money management can yield excellent results. The same is true of the fundamental approach. However, the middle road technical and fundamental, or a variety of a different technical systems all applied at one time, or a variety of different fundamental techniques all applied at one time is likely to produce poor results.

As you read on and attempt to find answers best suited to your needs, take into consideration the points I have raised in this chapter and do not make your decisions quickly. Finally, consider the possibility that a trading system may be a prerequisite to profitable trading. Successful traders are found at both ends of the continuum.

SUMMARY

The choice to follow fundamentals or technicals is a difficult one, but it is one that must be made on the basis of existing realities. While there has been much negative comment in recent years about the value of fundamentals, the fact remains that fundamentals are the ultimate factors that determine price. For the average speculator, however, the time, cost, and competition with large firms make fundamental analysis a difficult prospect. Technical trading approaches will work well, provided they are applied in a thorough and disciplined fashion. They are less costly, less time consuming, and more adaptable to today's computer technology. Hence, they are the method of choice for most speculators.

Chapter

3

What You Need to Know about Trendline Analysis

One of the most popular techniques of chart analysis is the use of trendlines. This method is used for determining levels of support and resistance, and buy and sell signals. This method has been around for a long time and has been studied by virtually every futures trader.

Trendlines appear to be effective, yet most traders are unfamiliar with a number of important aspects of trendline analysis. First, let's take a look at the definition of trendline analysis. The definition is important in order to keep our methods and procedures as operational as possible. This, in turn, reduces inconsistency and with it the degree of error.

My definition of a trendline is a line connecting a minimum of three nonconsecutive turning points on a chart. You can certainly see that a definition of this nature is so general that it leaves considerable room for interpretation (as well as misinterpretation). Let's expand the definition to include four essential types of trendlines with which you should be familiar.

1. **Support Line.** A line connecting at least three nonconsecutive turning points on a bar chart, slanting in a horizontal or upward direction and running under prices on the bar chart. Figure 3–1 shows several typical support lines.

2. **Resistance Line.** A resistance line consists of at least three nonconsecutive turning points running above the price on a bar chart and slanting downward or horizontally. Figure 3–2 illustrates several support and resistance lines. Figure 3–3 shows some resistance lines.

In addition to the two basic types of trendlines, there are two variations on trendlines.

Support Return Line: The extension of a support line into the future after the trendline has been penetrated, in order to determine possible future price resistance.

Resistance Return Line: The extension of a resistance line into the future once it has been penetrated by price in order to determine possible future support. Examples of support and resistance return lines are given in Figures 3–4, 3–5, and 3–6. Note how prices often come back to their return lines after penetration.

IMPLEMENTATION

Trendlines can be implemented in a trading program in a variety of ways. Traditionally, they are used as indications for buying and selling based upon the belief that once a trendline has been penetrated in one direction or another, an important price move is likely to continue in the direction of the penetration. Obviously, this is not always the case, but trendlines do appear to have validity as penetration points for buying and selling.

Trendlines have been used in several other ways. Many traders will turn bearish on the market when its support line has been penetrated to the downside. Prior to such penetration, however, traders will use the declines to the support line for going long on a market.

FIGURE 3-1 VARIOUS SUPPORT LINES
(Reprinted with permission of Commodity Quote Graphics)

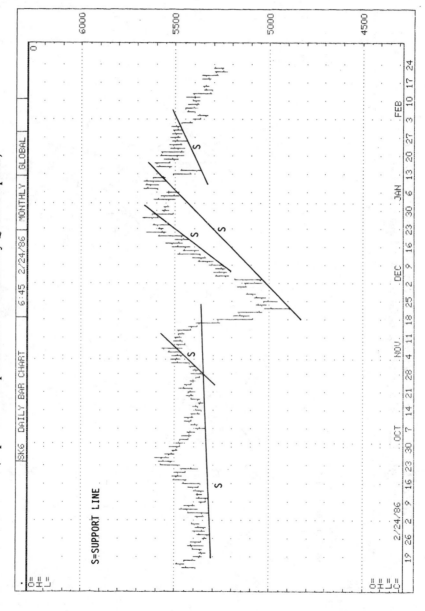

FIGURE 3–2   VARIOUS SUPPORT AND RESISTANCE LINES
(Reprinted with permission of Commodity Quote Graphics)

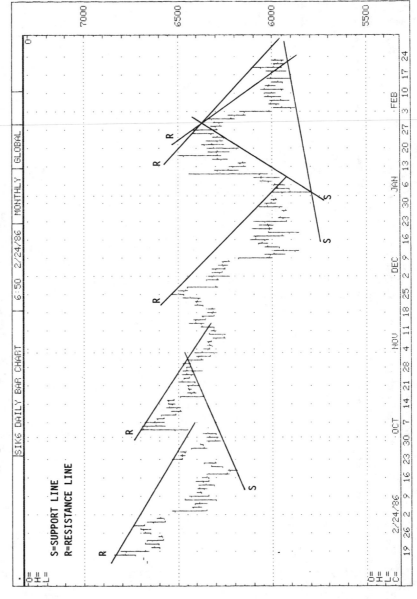

FIGURE 3-3   RESISTANCE LINES
(Reprinted with permission of Commodity Quote Graphics)

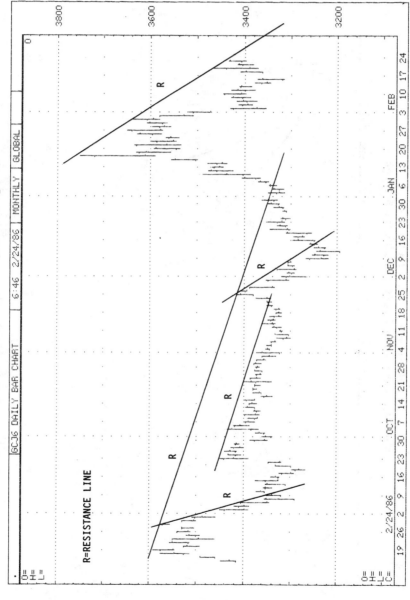

FIGURE 3-4 RETURN LINES
(Reprinted with permission of Commodity Quote Graphics)

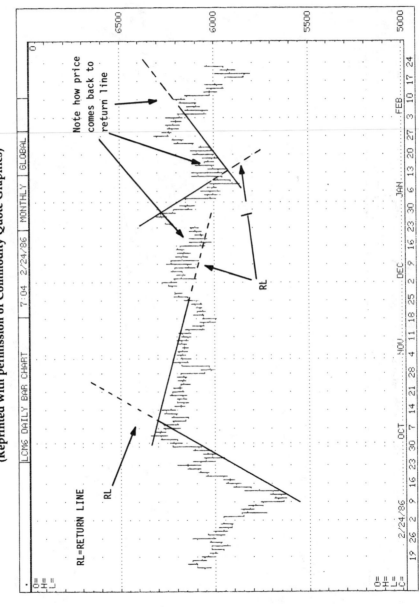

FIGURE 3–5 RETURN LINES
(Reprinted with permission of Commodity Quote Graphics)

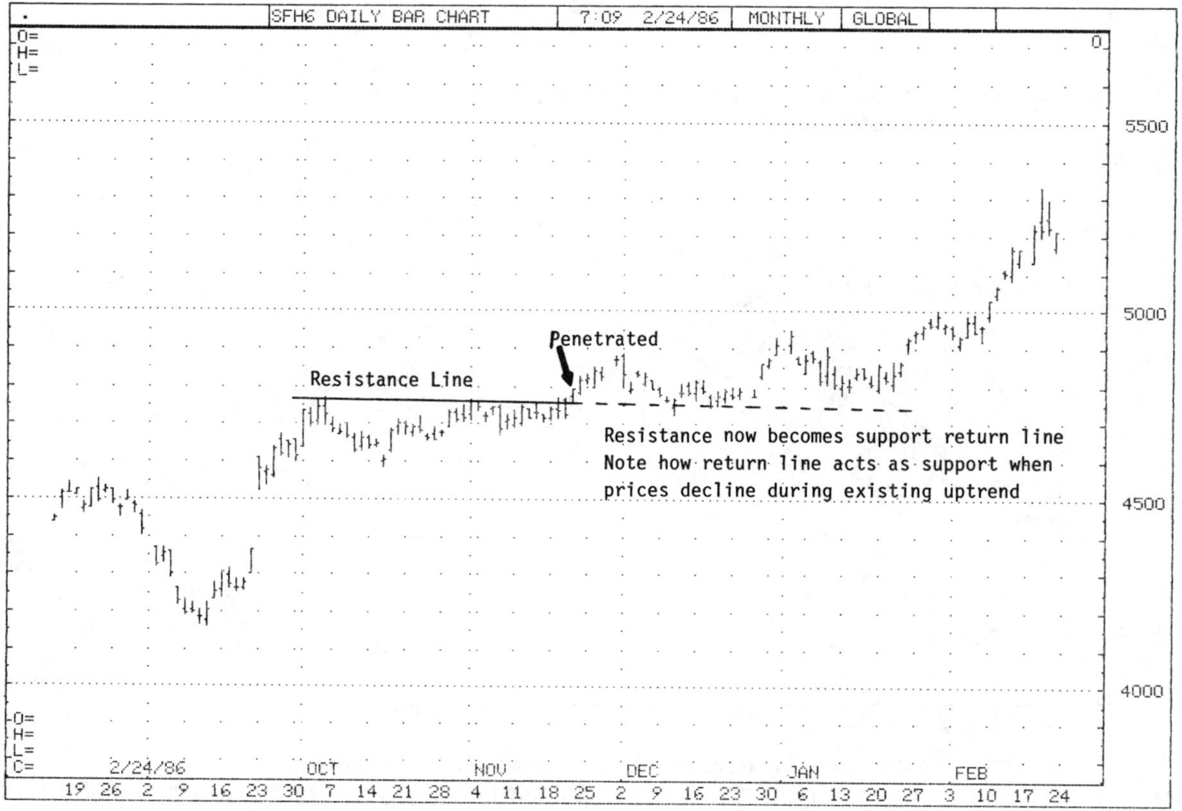
SFH6 DAILY BAR CHART
7:09 2/24/86
MONTHLY
GLOBAL
O=
H=
L=
C=
5500
5000
4500
4000
Resistance Line
Penetrated
Resistance now becomes support return line
Note how return line acts as support when
prices decline during existing uptrend
2/24/86
OCT
NOV
DEC
JAN
FEB
19 26 2 9 16 23 30 7 14 21 28 4 11 18 25 2 9 16 23 30 6 13 20 27 3 10 17 24

FIGURE 3-6   HOW RETURN LINES DEVELOP AS FUTURE SUPPORT AND/OR RESISTANCE
(Reprinted with permission of Commodity Quote Graphics)

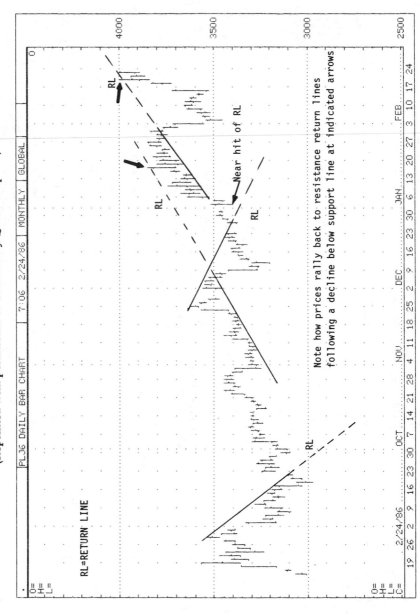

Alternatively, penetration of a resistance line is frequently taken to indicate a change in trend to the upside. Many traders will use the resistance line's points to establish short positions when a market rallies. Both techniques are commonly known and widely followed. It is difficult to state which procedure is the most reliable, but both have validity. Illustrations of all four applications are shown in Figures 3–7, 3–8, and 3–9.

SUGGESTIONS FOR APPLICATION

Many traders now prefer more sophisticated computer-generated signals. They have abandoned trendline methods in favor of these more complex but not necessarily effective systems. Some of the more intricate approaches will be discussed in later chapters. Based on my experience and observations in the markets, the trendline technique of buying on reactions to trendline support during an uptrend and selling on rallies to trendline resistance during a downtrend is a very effective technique.

The main focus in trendline analysis should not be on accurate signals, but rather on accurate interpretation of signals. There is a tendency by trendline followers to adapt trendlines to fit their particular needs or market bias. This temptation must be avoided. One should attempt to adhere as strictly as possible to trendline rules. Here are some suggestions as to how you might implement the trendline technique.

1. The single most important rule is to trade with the trend. This is the most frequently stated but most commonly misunderstood and overlooked aspect of successful speculation. Determining the major trend is not an especially difficult task, even for the novice trader. See Chapter 4 for detailed discussion on trend determination.

2. Assuming you have determined the major trend of prices and assuming that trend is up, the next step would be to draw support lines under the market.

3. Extend the trendlines into the future.

FIGURE 3-7 TRENDLINES AND SIGNALS
(Reprinted with permission of Commodity Quote Graphics)

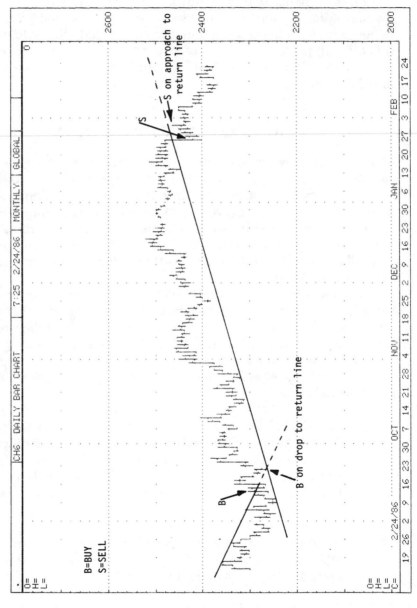

FIGURE 3-8   TRENDLINES AND SIGNALS
(Reprinted with permission of Commodity Quote Graphics)

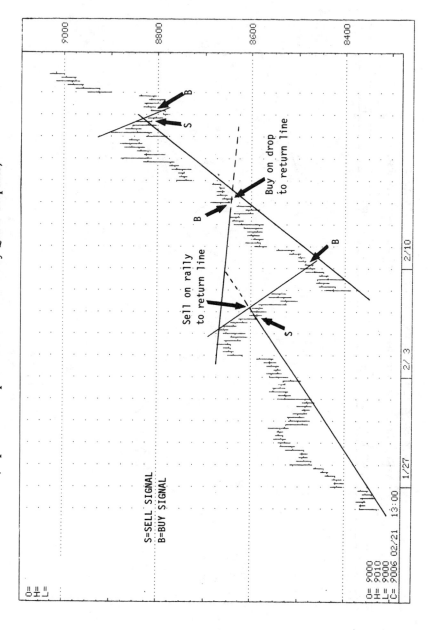

FIGURE 3-9   TRENDLINES AND SIGNALS
(Reprinted with permission of Commodity Quote Graphics)

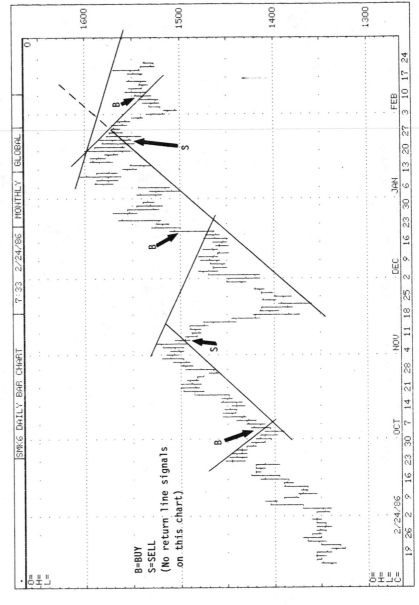

4. Determine the intersection point of trendline and price for the next market period (i.e., day, hour, etc.) Enter your price order slightly above the support line. I suggest a little leeway in order entry since many other traders will probably be entering their orders at or about the trendline price.

5. A good rule of thumb regarding stop losses is to liquidate your position as soon as your price has closed below the trendline, thereby negating its value as support and generating a reversing signal. Those willing to take a slightly greater risk can wait for two consecutive closings below the trendline, provided the first closing below the trendline does not exceed their maximum permissible per-trade losses (if such a limit is being used).

6. You can determine your objective in any of several ways. One technique is to reverse positions once a new trendline signal has formed. Another method is to sell your positions once a resistance line has been touched or approached. In the absence of a resistance line, other techniques could be used in liquidating a position, such as successively changing stops as the price continues to move in your favor (known as a trailing stop). The reverse procedure would hold true for selling short on the penetration of support.

As an aside, I would like you to remember that all my examples are drawn from real time and represent real market situations. I could have chosen very carefully many examples illustrating "ideal" or "perfect" situations. Since the perfect situation is the exception rather than the rule, I have given you as many current time examples as possible.

USE OF TRENDLINES ON INTRADAY DATA

Trendline analysis can also be effective on intraday price data. Ideally, a half-hour or 15-minute price chart of active markets is best for this purpose. Support, resistance, and trendline returns can be implemented on an intraday time scale. Illustrations of these techniques on intraday price charts are shown in Figures 3–10, 3–11, and 3–12.

Finally, as a point of information, Figures 3–13 and 3–14 show trendline analysis on a one-minute and five-minute open/high/low/close price chart for those individuals who are considering using trendline analysis on extremely short-term time frames.

SUMMARY

1. Trendline analysis is a viable technique that seems to have considerably less following in recent years due to the advent of more complex mathematical approaches requiring computer analysis.

2. There are at least four different types of trendline signals, each adaptable to specific situations.

3. Trendline analysis is probably a desirable technique since it is not practiced by as many traders today as has been the case in the past.

4. Trendline analysis can provide exit and entry points based on support and resistance within existing trends.

5. Trendline analysis is reasonably objective and can be applied in a fairly consistent fashion provided simple objective rules are followed.

6. Trendline trading does not require complex interpretations or sophisticated equipment. It is, therefore, ideal for the newcomer.

7. Trendline trading can be used on daily and/or intraday data.

FIGURE 3–10   TRENDLINE SIGNALS ON INTRADAY DATA
(Reprinted with permission of Commodity Quote Graphics)

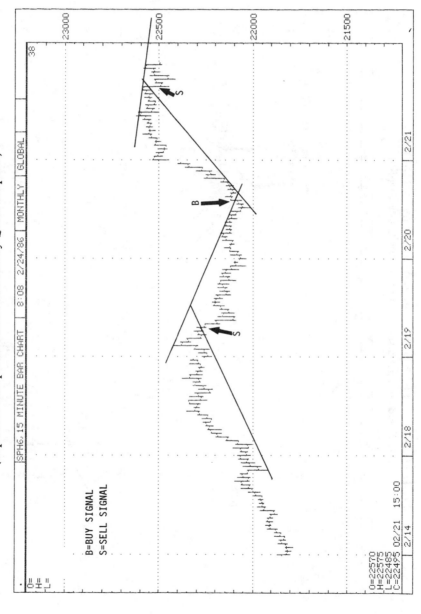

FIGURE 3–11   TRENDLINE SIGNALS ON INTRADAY DATA
(Reprinted with permission of Commodity Quote Graphics)

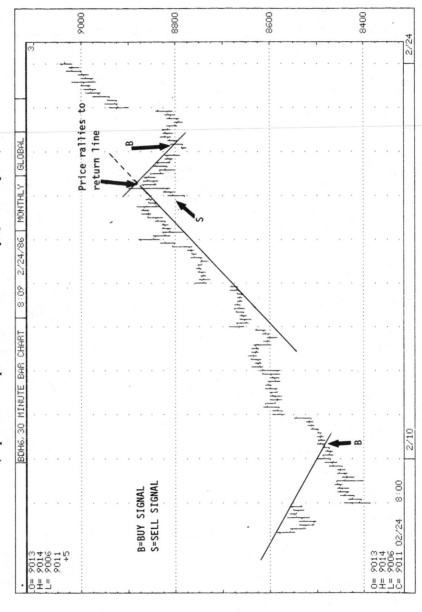

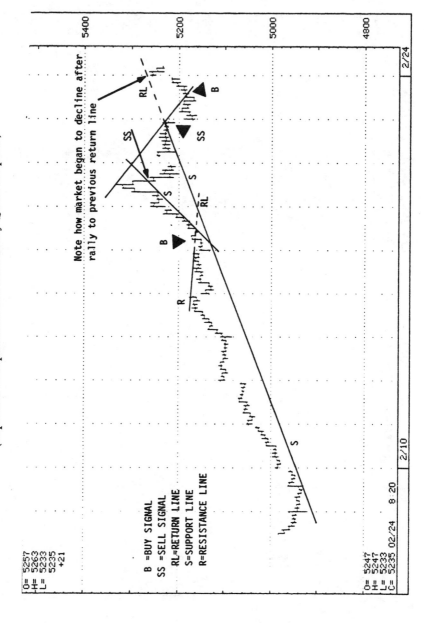

FIGURE 3–12   TRENDLINE SIGNALS ON INTRADAY DATA
(Reprinted with permission of Commodity Quote Graphics)

FIGURE 3-13 TRENDLINE SIGNALS ON ONE-MINUTE CHART
(Reprinted with permission of Commodity Quote Graphics)

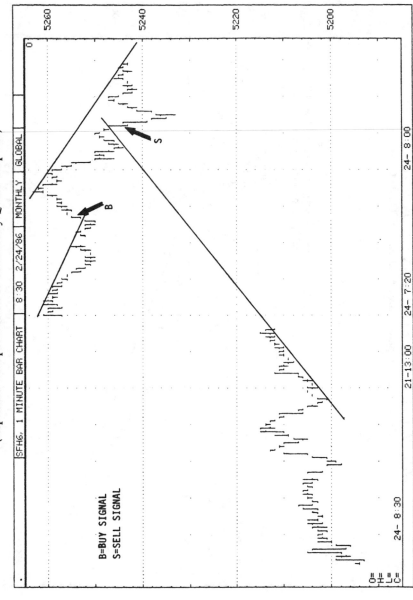

FIGURE 3–14   TRENDLINE SIGNALS ON FIVE-MINUTE CHART
(Reprinted with permission of Commodity Quote Graphics)

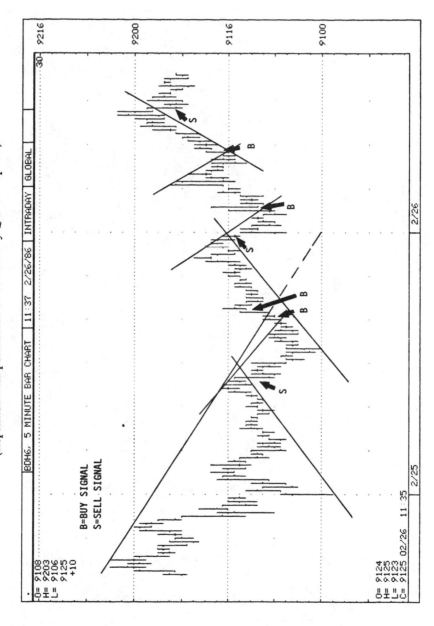

Chapter

4

What You Should Know about Cycles

The cyclic method of analysis and forecasting has its roots in the work of Edward R. Dewey, founder of The Foundation for the Study of Cycles. Dewey's original work was in the cash commodity markets, as well as in the stock market. With the advent and accessibility of computer technology, the use of price cycles has become more popular. Yet, due to the complexity of cycle analysis, it still does not have many followers today.

Let me preface my remarks about price cycles by saying that the cyclic technique is somewhat complicated and not recommended for the new trader. Though I have been a proponent of cyclic trading for many years, I can say in all honesty that the application of cycles is more challenging than simply demonstrating their existence.

It is relatively simple to find price cycles, even if your experience in the futures markets is limited. A number of techniques may be employed to find cycles in futures and futures options. Some of the basic timing indicators used with cyclic price patterns can help you do extremely well. However, the intricacies of cyclic analysis are

such that a commitment must be made and kept in order to achieve
lasting success.

WHAT IS A CYCLE?

Stated simply, a price cycle is the tendency for price to repeat up and
down trends in a relatively predictable fashion over a prescribed
period of time. In other words, it is possible to state with fairly good
accuracy that corn prices have a price cycle of approximately 5.7
years. This price cycle is illustrated in Figure 4–1. Within the 5.7-year
price cycle for corn, there are also 30- to 34-month price cycles.

Price cycles are measured low to low, high to high, or low to
high. Various types of measurements are possible. A more thorough
understanding of price cycles, timing indicators, and cyclic theories
may be obtained from my book, *The Handbook of Commodity Cycles: A
Window on Time.*[1] Examples of various price cycles are provided in
Figures 4–1 through 4–5.

MANY DIFFERENT CYCLES

Futures and cash prices demonstrate many different cyclic lengths
ranging from the ultra-long term to the ultra-short term. On the
short-term end of the spectrum, we have the approximately four- to
five-day cycle in silver prices. On the long-term end of the continuum, we have the approximate 54-year cycle found in most commodity prices. This is about the longest cycle commodity traders study.

For the purpose of trading, cycle lengths from as long as 9 to 11
months to as short as 14 days are preferable. Most trading will likely
be done on the basis of the approximate 25- to 32-day cycles. Figure
4-5 shows a listing of recent cycle low/high dates, cycle lengths, and
specific markets. Note that these are subject to change.

Price cycles are not perfect; they can vary considerably in length.
At times there will be an inversion of cyclic highs and lows, with tops

---

1   J.Bernstein, *The Handbook of Commodity Cycles: A Window on Time* (New York:
        John Wiley & Sons, 1982)

FIGURE 4–1 5.7-YEAR CORN PRICE CYCLE (Arrows Show Longer Term Cycles)

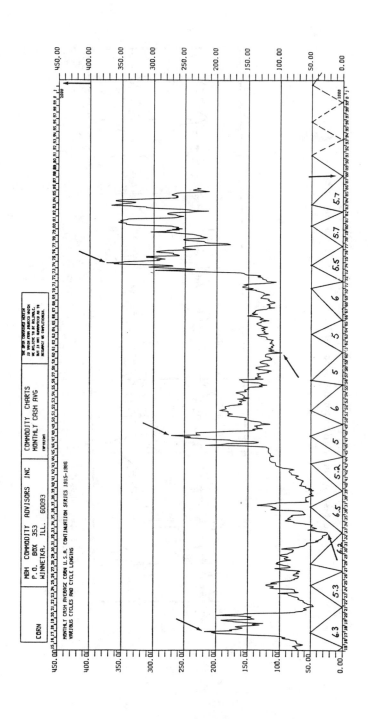

CORN

MBH COMMODITY ADVISORS INC
P.O. BOX 353
WINNETKA, ILL. 60093

COMMODITY CHARTS
MONTHLY CASH AVG

MONTHLY CASH AVERAGE CORN U.S.A. CONTINUATION SERIES 1915-1986
VARIOUS CYCLES AND CYCLE LENGTHS

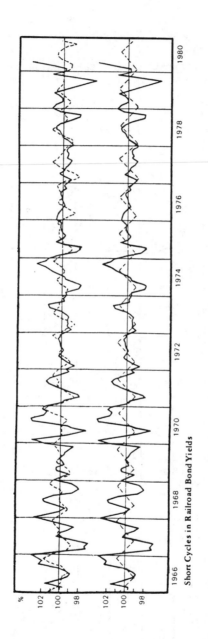

FIGURE 4-2   PRICE CYCLES IN BOND YIELDS
(Courtesy of Foundation for the Study of Cycles, 124 S. Highland, Pittsburgh, PA)

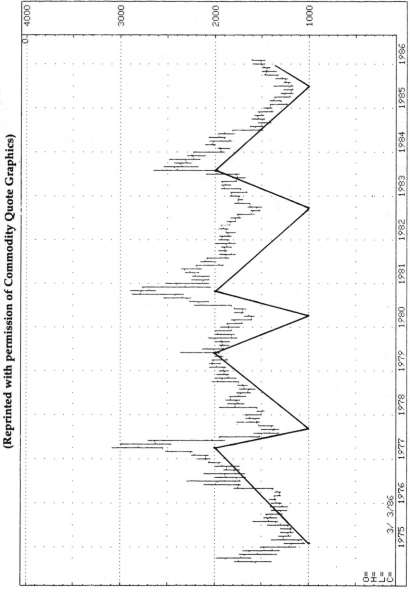

FIGURE 4-3   PRICE CYCLES IN SOYBEAN MEAL FUTURES
(Reprinted with permission of Commodity Quote Graphics)

FIGURE 4-4   APPROXIMATE 20-MONTH CYCLE IN CATTLE FUTURES
(Reprinted with permission of Commodity Quote Graphics)

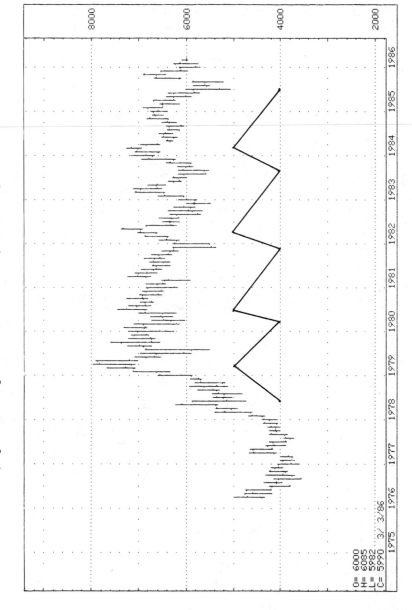

FIGURE 4–5
SAMPLE CYCLE LOW/HIGH DATES,
LENGTHS AND TRENDS

MARKET	MONTH	LT	HIGH / LOW		IT	HIGH / LOW		ST	HIGH / LOW	
LvCattle	Apr	10.2	1985	1985	45	12/85	07/85	32	01/27	02/19
LvHogs	Apr	1.7	1982	1985	45	12/85	09/85	28	01/27	02/18
PkBellies	May	1.7	1982	1985	45	12/85	08/85	28	01/27	due
Corn	May	2.8	1983	due	43	04/85	09/85	54	12/18	due
Oats	May	3.0	1983	due	43	03/85	due	40	12/31	02/20
Soybeans	May	2.8	1983	due	46	03/85	11/85	54	01/07	due
Soymeal	May	2.8	1983	1985	46	10/84	07/85	54	01/09	02/04
Soyoil	May	4.1	due	1984	46	04/85	12/85	54	12/17	due
Wheat	May	2.8	1983	1985	55	04/85	08/85	54	12/12	02/20
Cotton	May	5.9	1980	----	43	04/85	08/85	43	01/22	01/30
HtgOil	May	---	----	----	41	11/85	06/85	28	12/30	due
Lumber	May	4.0	1983	due	42	05/85	08/85	26	12/16	02/05
Sugar	May	6.2	1980	1985	56	10/85	06/85	56	12/02	01/14
O.J.	May	3.1	1984	due	35	01/85	due	60	12/17	02/24
Cocoa	May	3.7	1978	1982	44	12/85	03/85	54	01/07	due
Coffee	May	6.7	1977	1981	55	02/85	07/85	30	01/07	02/04
Copper	May	5.9	1980	1985	45	04/85	09/85	38	01/14	02/11
Silver	May	5.5	1980	1982	45	03/85	12/85	38	01/16	due
Gold	Apr	6.3	1980	1982	45	08/85	12/85	38	01/16	02/14*
Platinum	Apr	5.5	1980	1982	40	11/85	03/85	38	02/25*	02/04
Palladium	Jun	5.5	1980	1982	40	08/85	07/85	38	01/16	02/04*
TBills	Jun	4.5	due	1981	21	due	03/85	29	02/04	02/20
TBonds	Jun	4.5	due	1981	21	due	07/85	29	due	02/20
SwFranc	Jun	3.0	1980	due	41	due	02/85	41	due	01/13
DMark	Jun	3.0	1980	due	41	due	02/85	41	due	01/13
BrPound	Jun	6.1	1980	due	43	due	02/85	42	due	02/04
JYen	Jun	5.9	1978	due	43	due	02/85	42	due	12/03
CDollar	Jun	5.9	1980	due	21	10/85	09/85	21	02/24*	02/04
S&PIndex	Jun	4.0	due	1982	23	01/86	due	23	Uncertain	

Explanatory Notes: LT=Long Term Cycle Length measured in years and fractions. IT=
Intermediate Term Cycle Length measured in weeks. ST=Short Term Cycle Length measured
in market days. All cycles are measured in weeks. ST cycles are measured in market
days not calendar days. Cycle lengths are approximate and subject to change over time.
Dates listed are tentative and subject to change when more data becomes available.
"---" indicates that our research has not yet revealed any cycles of reliability or that
our data base is too limited. Cycles are not necessarily symmetrical.

being made when lows should be made. This tends to occur at major turning points in the markets. For the purposes of this discussion, we will concern ourselves with 9- to 11-month cycles and 14- to 60-day cycles.

APPLICATION OF THE THEORY

The application of the price cycles to futures trading consists of three elements: (1) cycle projections, (2) projection, and (3) timing entry.

First, if you do not know the cycle length for a given market, you can research it in any of several ways. There are computer programs that will help you find cycles by matching dates and cycle lengths and testing them in the past, as well as projecting them into the future. Once you know the cycle length, the second element is to forecast the next approximate high or low. This is done simply by counting forward in time and establishing a time frame or time window during which the cycle should ideally top or bottom. See Figure 4–6 for an illustration. Once you have determined the ideal time frame of the next low or high, what I call the "time window," you will wait for the market to enter this time frame and, regardless of price, you act upon the timing indicator or timing signal, which allows you to enter with the anticipation of high probability of success.

TIMING INDICATORS

The use of timing indicators is possible during the optimum time frame for a top or bottom in the cycle. I have used several traditional and not-so-traditional tools. On the traditional side, we have the three basic timing signals I advanced in greater detail in my book, *The Handbook of Commodity Cycles: A Window on Time.*[2]

The three basic indicators are shown in Figures 4–7, 4–8, and 4–9.

---

2   J. Bernstein, *The Handbook of Commodity Cycles.*

FIGURE 4-6   APPROXIMATE 16-MONTH CYCLE IN SWISS FRANC FUTURES
(Reprinted with permission of Commodity Quote Graphics)

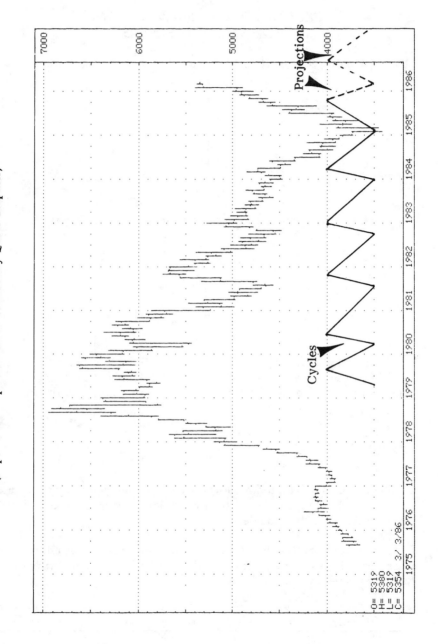

FIGURE 4–7
BASIC INDICATORS—UPSIDE AND
DOWNSIDE REVERSALS

Upside Reversal: Used for buying in cycle low time

Downside Reversal: Used for selling in cycle high time

If H_1 = high of day 1   And H_2 = high of day 2
       L_1 = low of day 1 L_2 = low of day 2
And C_1 = closing price of day 1 C_2 = closing price of day 2

Then upside reversal is
$$L_2 < L_1 \text{ and } C_2 > C_1 = R\,+$$
The downside reversal is
$$H_2 > H_1 \text{ and } C_2 < C_1 = R\,-$$

Upside Reversal (R +) If today's low price is less than yesterday's low price and today's closing price is more than yesterday's closing price, then a daily upside reversal has been made.

Downside Reversal (R –) If today's high price is more than yesterday's high price and today's closing price is less than yesterday's closing price, then a daily downside reversal has been made.

FIGURE 4–8
BASIC INDICATORS—LOW/HIGH CLOSE AND
HIGH/LOW CLOSE TIMING SIGNALS

High Low Close Used for Selling in Cycle High Time (HLC)

Low High Close Signal Used for Buying in Cycle Low Time (LHC)

Close on low is defined as close at or within 10% of low. Close on high is defined as close at or within 10% of high. Both signals must occur on consecutive time periods in the time frame for the cycle turn.

FIGURE 4–9
BASIC INDICATORS—3H/3L TIMING INDICATORS

3H Indicator Used for Buying in Cycle Low Time

BUY   BUY   BUY   BUY

3L Indicator Used for Selling in Cycle High Time

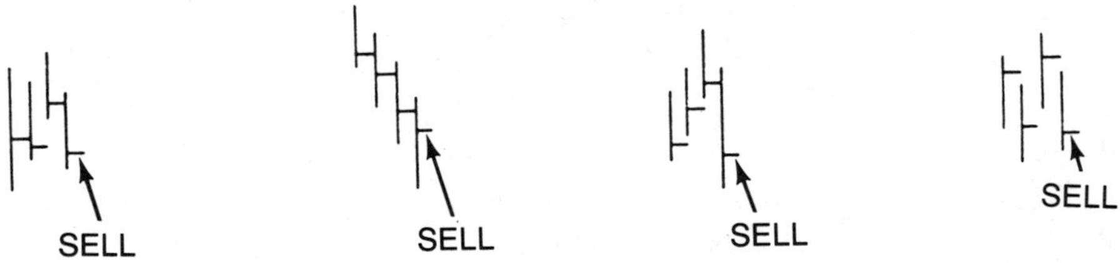

SELL   SELL   SELL   SELL

3H is defined as 4th close above highest of last three closes.
3L is defined as 4th close below lowest of last three closes.

CYCLIC TRADING RULES

Although there are many different approaches to cycles and applications of cyclic theory, some general rules can help you in your study and application of cycles in the futures markets. Here is a summary of those rules:

1. Find a market that has reliable cycles. Currently, some of these cycles are the 20–23-week cycle in stock index futures, the approximately 14-day cycle in stock index futures, the 50–60-day cycle in soybean futures, the 9–11-month cycle in all grain and livestock markets, the approximately 28-day cycle in silver and gold, and the approximately 32-day cycle in interest rate futures. As market conditions change, cycles become more or less reliable and certain markets begin to exhibit better or worse cyclic tendencies. Therefore, continue to study the markets in order to isolate markets best traded using cycles.

2. Do not attempt to trade more than two or three markets at once based on cycles.

3. Do not duplicate markets. What I mean here is don't trade several different markets that are closely related and that follow the same basic cycles (i.e., silver and gold, cattle and hogs, soybeans and soybean meal).

4. Once you have determined the above information, keep your price charts up to date and mark your cycles according to the rules provided in this chapter.

5. Project the next cyclic top or bottom as I have illustrated (Figure 4–5).

6. Once you have entered the ideal cyclic time frame of a top or bottom, examine timing signals and/or various timing indicators to pinpoint as closely as possible the next market turn.

7. Use stop losses specific to each trading signal.

8. Attempt to develop a trailing stop procedure by which you continually adjust your stop once you are in a profitable position. This is done so that not too much profit is lost back to the market if prices turn against you.

LIMITATIONS OF TRADING WITH CYCLICAL INDICATORS

While cycles are an excellent tool for spotting long-term trends and potential changes in trend, timing can be a difficult proposition due to the variability in the length of cycles. While there *are* methods such as spectral analysis and Fourier analysis which can help pinpoint the time frame for cyclical turns, they have their limitations as well.

SUMMARY

The cyclic method of futures trading is viable, but not recommended for novice traders. Used with an effective approach to timing and a sensible method of money management, this approach is capable of generating good profits over the short and long term. The use of futures-options can improve cyclic timing by allowing more time within the ideal top and bottom time frames.

Chapter

5

What You Need to Know about Moving Averages

In 1955, Richard Donchain advanced the notion that a different type of trendline could be used to establish buy and sell signals, as well as indications of support and resistance. Rather than the familiar (straight-line) trend method, Donchain advanced the notion that a moving average of price could be determined in order to provide market timing indicators.

A moving average is a simple mathematical manipulation of raw data that provides up-to-date or moving indications of market activity. Instead of examining price highs and lows for the entire history of the current contract, a moving average constantly progresses and examines only a defined segment of time, particularly in the recent past.

A 10-day moving average, for example, will only look at prices for the last 10 days, ignoring what has transpired before. In so doing, it provides a more sensitive measure by taking an average of the last ten days worth of prices, and on the 11th day dropping the oldest day in the data and recalculating the average with the current daily data. At any given point, only 10 days of data are used. However, they are the most recent 10 days.

Theoretically, price movement above the moving average is considered bullish. If a market has been in an uptrend and then falls below the moving average line, this is taken to indicate a probable change in trend from bullish to bearish. Conversely if the market has been moving down (i.e., below moving average) and if it then crosses above its moving average, this is taken to be a bullish signal.

Although relatively simple to understand and straightforward in its construction and interpretation, the moving average has undergone many changes both in construction and application during the last 30 years. In only a few cases have the changes and additional effort been fruitful. Figures 5–1, 5–2, 5–3, and 5–4 show several markets plotted with moving averages of different lengths. You will observe that the vertical lines show the opening high/low price bars and that the dotted smooth line shows the moving average plot. Observe my notes and comments.

Although the selection of one moving average as a means of timing entry and exit is certainly a technique which appears to have potential, it has been found that two moving averages, and perhaps three, tend to serve the purpose better. Whereas, one moving average will only indicate the trend over a specific length of time, the addition of one or two moving average indicators could significantly improve results by providing several measures of market strength or weakness.

Theoretically, buy signals are generated when two moving average lines cross in the upward direction, and sell signals are generated when two moving averages cross in the downward direction (see Figures 5–5 and 5–6). Finally, a third moving average could be added to further verify timing or to provide more evidence of a change in trend.

The application of various moving averages to determine buy and sell indications has received considerable study over the years. Certain combinations in certain markets are optimum, and other combinations do not appear to be particularly fruitful. Specifically, the 4-, 9-, and 18-day moving averages seem to work best together. Figures 5–7, 5–8, and 5–9 show this combination, and the signals that can be generated from its application.

FIGURE 5-1   MOVING AVERAGES PLOTTED
(Reprinted with permission of Commodity Quote Graphics)

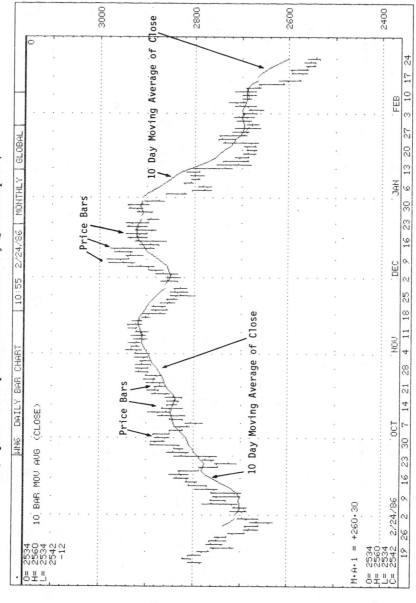

FIGURE 5-2   MOVING AVERAGES -PLOTTED
(Reprinted with permission of Commodity Quote Graphics)

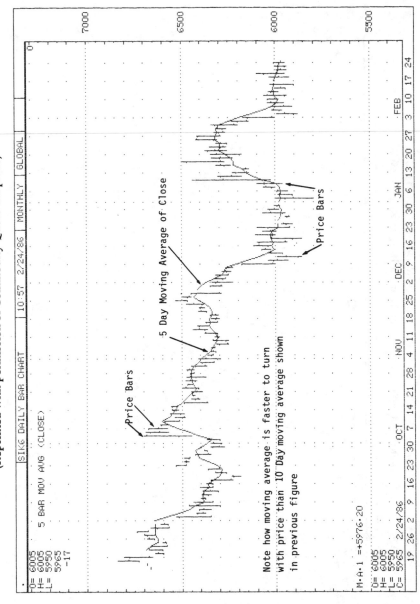

FIGURE 5–3   MOVING AVERAGES PLOTTED
(Reprinted with permission of Commodity Quote Graphics)

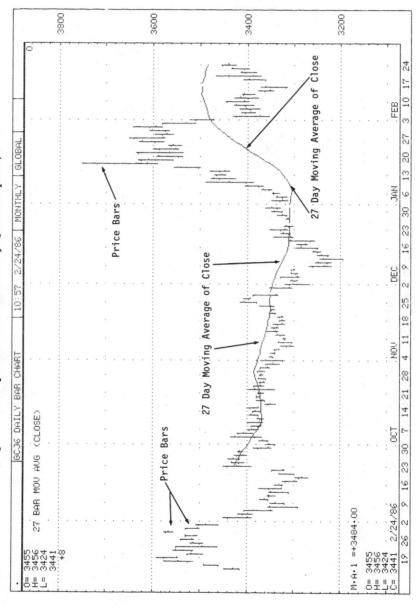

FIGURE 5-4   MOVING AVERAGES PLOTTED
(Reprinted with permission of Commodity Quote Graphics)

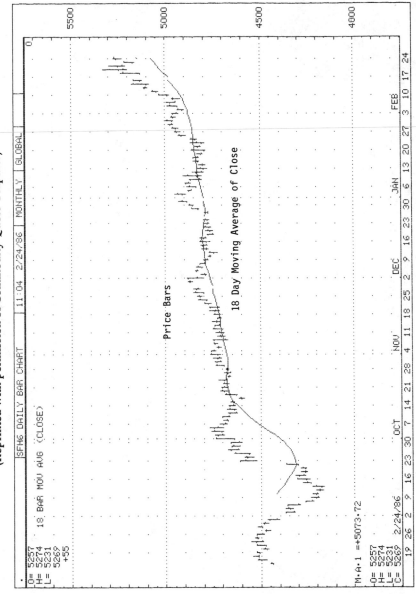

FIGURE 5-5 MOVING AVERAGES LINES CROSSING
(Reprinted with permission of Commodity Quote Graphics)

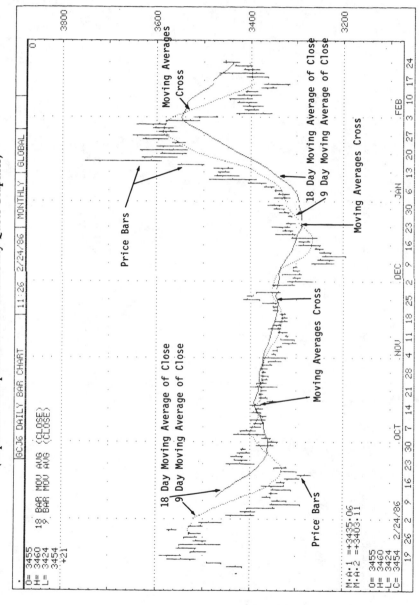

FIGURE 5–6   MOVING AVERAGES LINES CROSSING
(Reprinted with permission of Commodity Quote Graphics)

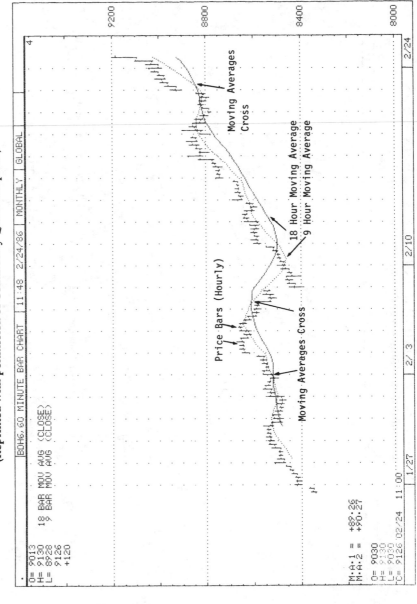

FIGURE 5-7   4-, 9-, AND 18-DAY MOVING AVERAGES
(Reprinted with permission of Commodity Quote Graphics)

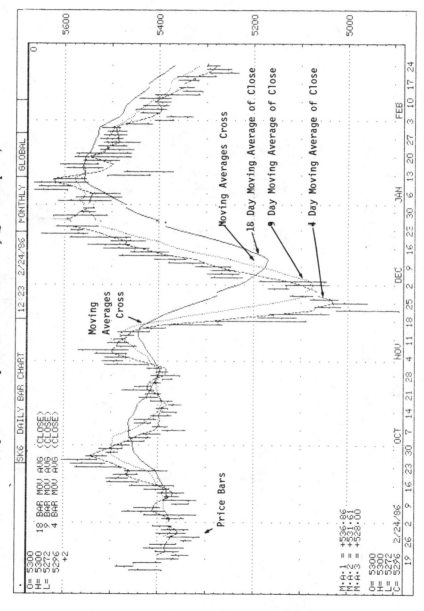

FIGURE 5-8   4-, 9-, AND 18-DAY MOVING AVERAGES
(Reprinted with permission of Commodity Quote Graphics)

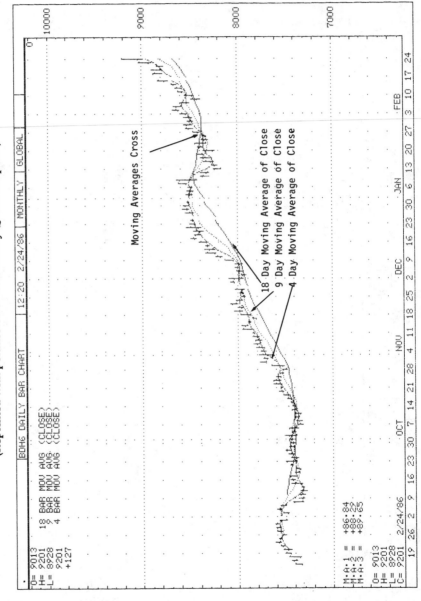

FIGURE 5–9 4-, 9-, AND 18-DAY MOVING AVERAGES
(Reprinted with permission of Commodity Quote Graphics)

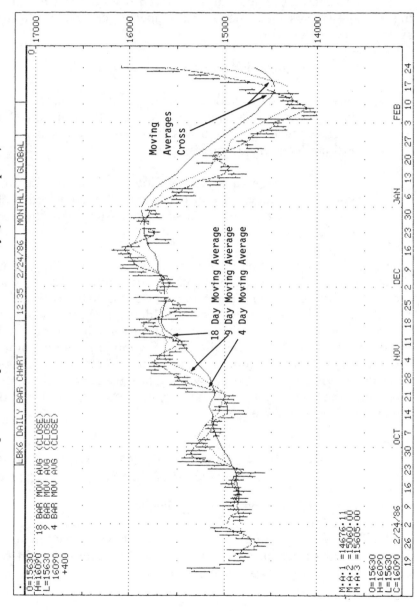

Moving average signals are frequently used by money managers and speculators. Their popularity is derived from the fact that moving average signals meet many of the specific criteria of effective systems. These are:

1.   Moving average signals are specific and objective.

2.   Moving average signals can keep you in the market at all times: closing out a long, going short, and covering a short when going long. This is valuable, since you will have a position when major moves begin.

3.   Moving averages are trend-following systems. In other words, when a good trend is in effect, the likelihood of the moving average having a position consistent with the trend is very high.

Whatever combination of moving averages you may be using, the fact remains that moving averages are mechanical and easily implemented. Unfortunately, in certain types of markets moving averages do not do well. These are primarily sideways or choppy markets in which prices may work back and forth in a small or large range, but over such a brief period of time that the moving average indicators are almost constantly out of phase with market activity. In such cases the moving average system will not fare well and, indeed, may fare worse than most systems. However, in a trending market, moving average systems shine.

REVIEWING THE MOVING AVERAGE INDICATOR SIGNALS

1.   Compute the moving average lengths.

2.   Buy when all three moving averages have crossed in an upward direction. (If using one moving average, then buy when price closes above the M.A.)

3. Sell and sell short when all three moving averages have crossed in a downward direction. (If using one moving average, then sell when price closes below the M.A.)

4. Moving average systems are based on reversals. In other words, when a long position is closed out, a short position is entered. When a short position is closed out, a long position is entered.

Moving average systems can be valuable to the new trader. Though they may result in greater than acceptable risk, they do assist with self-discipline and money management. Before you consider using moving averages for trading, study this approach very thoroughly. There are many variations on this theme, some much better than others.

LIMITATIONS OF MOVING AVERAGES

There are two significant limitations to the use of moving averages. They are:

1. Low accuracy results in large drawdowns. This means your account equity can drop significantly due to a string of losing trades. By the time the system turns higher you will be out of capital.

2. Moving average systems are often reversing systems; that is, they require you to reverse your position from short to long and vice versa. This means you do not know your stop loss before entering a trade. This limits your ability to determine risk before you trade. And this is not a good idea, particularly for the new trader.

SUMMARY

The general aspects of moving averages were discussed. Some specifics regarding moving average techniques were reviewed and
illustrated. Strengths and weaknesses of traditional moving average
systems were reviewed. The moving average systems available today
are much more sophisticated and well-tested than they have been in
the past. Consistent application of moving average techniques has
validity as a successful methodology for technical traders. The use of
such systems should not be discounted by novice traders inasmuch
as these systems are specific, mechanical, trend following, and relatively simple to follow. Though there can be large drawdowns and
periods of persistent losses in zig zag ("whipsaw") type markets, the
potential of moving average systems in trending markets is tremendous.

Chapter

6

What You Need to Know about Seasonality

Another form of cyclical price movement is seasonality. Seasonality refers to the tendency of prices to move in certain directions at certain times of the year. Some seasonal price tendencies are extremely reliable, having occurred in excess of 90 percent of the time over a span of many years. Other seasonals are less reliable.

In recent years, the popularity of trading in anticipation of seasonal price tendencies has grown partly as a result of computer use in analyzing large amounts of statistics used to isolate these tendencies. There are three different types of seasonal tendencies: (1) cash seasonality, (2) futures seasonality, and (3) futures spread seasonality.

CASH SEASONALITY

Each cash commodity market has its own seasonal tendency. If we study cash commodity prices over an extended period of time on a month-to-month change basis, we find that during certain months of the year, price tends to top, whereas during other months price tends to bottom. Furthermore, during certain times of the year uptrends are common while during other times of the year downtrends are common. Seasonality was described by W. D. Gann in some of his publications as far back as 1932. References are listed at the end of this chapter. The technique of constructing or calculating a seasonal price tendency chart is very simple. The procedure is as follows:

1. List the monthly cash average prices in tabular form.

2. Calculate the differences from one month to the next for the entire period of data.

3. List the differences in columns according to month, for example January to February differences, February to March differences, March to April differences.

4. Add the month-to-month differences for each year back to the start of your data.

5. Take the average of your differences.

6. Plot the first average. Add it to the second average of difference and plot this figure. Do so until you have plotted all 12 months of differences.

7. Calculate the percentage of time during the history of your data that prices are up or down for a given month. What you will arrive at is a chart that looks like Figure 6–1.

Cash price seasonal tendencies will allow you to determine when markets are likely to be their strongest or weakest, and when markets usually top or bottom. They do not, however, have much applicability for the short-term trader. Their primary use is for the producer, hedger, or long-term trader. Figures 6–1 through 6–5 show some cash seasonals for various markets.

FIGURE 6–1
CASH SEASONALITY IN WHEAT (1936-1983)

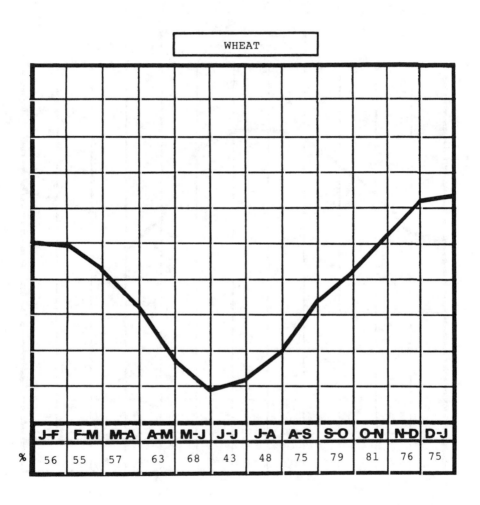

WHEAT

	J-F	F-M	M-A	A-M	M-J	J-J	J-A	A-S	S-O	O-N	N-D	D-J
%	56	55	57	63	68	43	48	75	79	81	76	75

FIGURE 6–2
CASH SEASONAL PRICE TENDENCY IN SOYBEANS

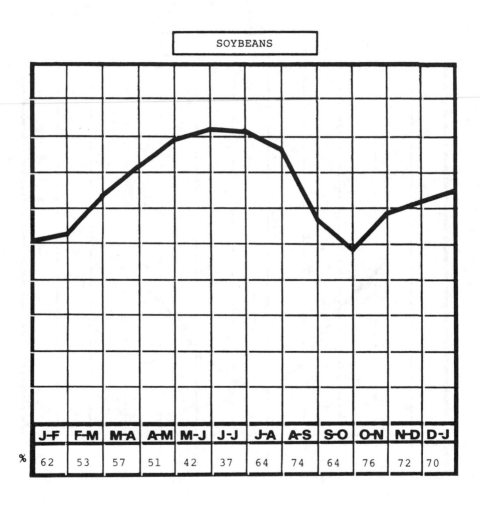

SOYBEANS

J-F	F-M	M-A	A-M	M-J	J-J	J-A	A-S	S-O	O-N	N-D	D-J
62	53	57	51	42	37	64	74	64	76	72	70

%

FIGURE 6–3
CASH SEASONAL PRICE TENDENCY IN COPPER

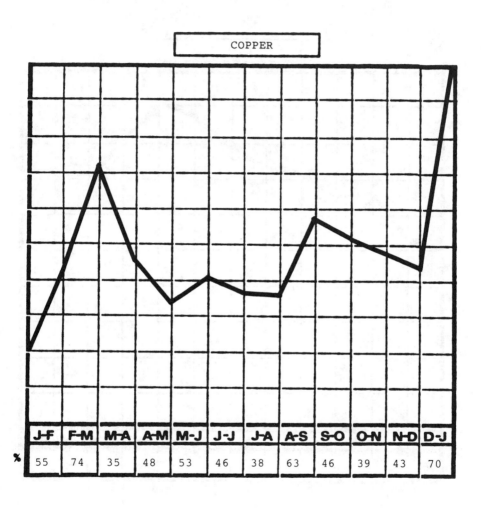

	J-F	F-M	M-A	A-M	M-J	J-J	J-A	A-S	S-O	O-N	N-D	D-J
%	55	74	35	48	53	46	38	63	46	39	43	70

FIGURE 6–4
CASH SEASONAL PRICE TENDENCY IN LUMBER

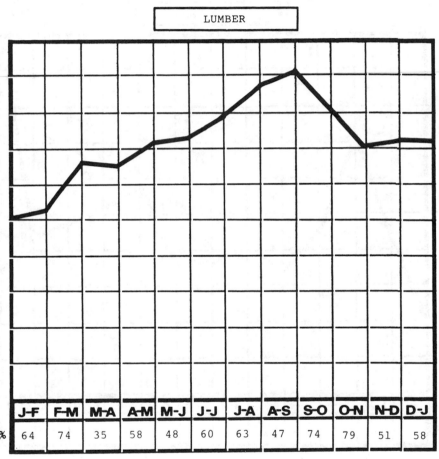

LUMBER

	J-F	F-M	M-A	A-M	M-J	J-J	J-A	A-S	S-O	O-N	N-D	D-J
%	64	74	35	58	48	60	63	47	74	79	51	58

FIGURE 6–5
CASH SEASONAL PRICE TENDENCY IN CATTLE
(BEEF STEERS)

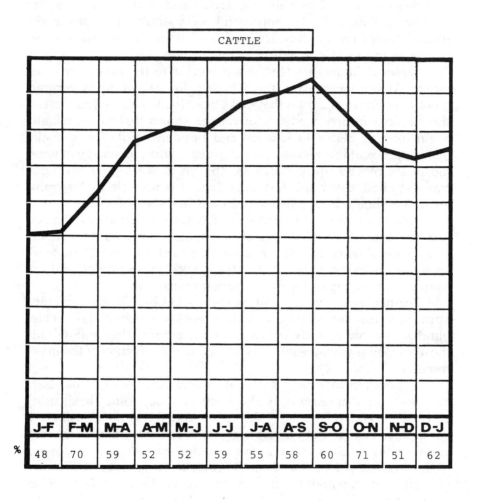

CATTLE											
J-F	F-M	M-A	A-M	M-J	J-J	J-A	A-S	S-O	O-N	N-D	D-J
48	70	59	52	52	59	55	58	60	71	51	62

%

SEASONAL FUTURES TENDENCIES

The use of seasonal futures tendencies on a week-to-week or day-to-day basis can be more useful to the short-term trader. Several approaches can be used in analyzing weekly and daily seasonal futures tendencies. Essentially, the approach is very similar to what was described earlier for monthly seasonal tendencies in the cash market. However, in this case weekly or daily data are used.

Seasonal futures tendencies are specific to the futures contract month. When we analyze the statistics for each futures contract month, we arrive at a chart that looks like Figure 6–6. As you can see, the seasonal futures tendency of copper shows that prices usually begin moving higher in January and peak in April. The statistics inside the box at the bottom of the chart show the percentage of times the prices moved up or down for the given week over the time-frame studied. Given this historical data, it is possible to determine when one should ideally be long or short in a given market.

This is not to say that the seasonals shown will always be correct. Certainly there is a degree of probability. However, they do tell you the usual market tendency at even times of the year. These tendencies can help you to stay out of the market when needed and can keep you on the right side of the market more often.

Furthermore, you can "filter" the market by using a combined approach. Instead of following the weekly seasonal tendencies blindly, you could study the major market trend, then follow only those weekly seasonal readings which go in the direction of the major trend.

In addition to weekly seasonal futures tendencies, it has been demonstrated that seasonality also exists on a day-to-day basis using early futures data. Figure 6–7 shows some of the statistics using calendar days change from December cotton futures. Observe that my arrows point to days that the given market has been up or down a high percentage of the time. Such short-term seasonal statistics can be generated on all markets with an appropriately long data base. However, the weekly approach I have described is best suited to most traders.

FIGURE 6–6   CASH SEASONAL FUTURES TENDENCY, JULY COPPER (1967–1984)

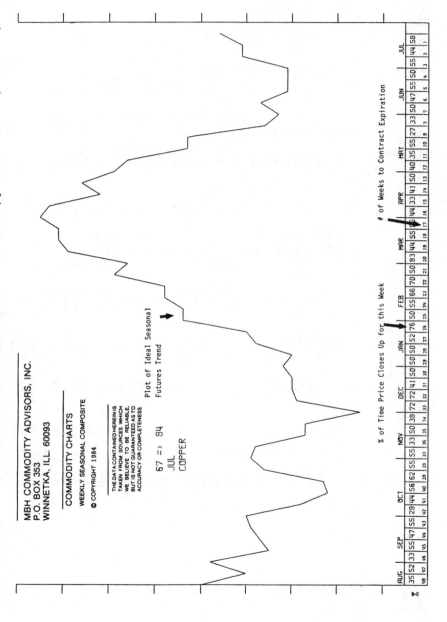

FIGURE 6–7 SEASONAL STATISTICS USING CALENDAR DAYS—Percent of Time Price was Up or Down for Given Market on Indicated Calendar Day During Time Period Studied in December Cotton Futures—Arrows Show High Readings

DATE	% Days Up	% Days Down	Avg. +	Avg. -		DATE	% Days Up	% Days Down	Avg. +	Avg. -
SEP 22	50	50	0.35	0.57		OCT 25	63	37	0.66	0.85
SEP 23	50	50	0.27	0.36		OCT 26	50	50	0.23	0.55
SEP 24	58	42	0.48	0.87		OCT 27	53	47	0.38	0.36
SEP 25	50	50	0.54	0.75		OCT 28	58	42	0.24	0.48
SEP 26	41	59	0.30	0.69		OCT 29	58	42	0.54	0.37
SEP 27	58	42	0.72	0.26		OCT 30	66	34	0.41	0.78
SEP 28	66	34	0.31	0.50		OCT 31	50	50	0.49	0.26
SEP 29	53	47	0.36	0.46						
SEP 30	58	42	1.00	0.18		NOV 1	25	75 ▶	0.72	0.65
						NOV 2	40	60	0.34	0.31
OCT 1	50	50	0.52	0.89		NOV 3	33	67	0.52	0.60
OCT 2	50	50	0.46	0.85		NOV 4	66	34	0.53	0.06
OCT 3	66	34	0.61	0.53		NOV 5	40	60	0.70	0.39
OCT 4	50	50	0.12	0.45		NOV 6	63	37	0.22	0.67
OCT 5	83 ▶	17	0.40	0.08		NOV 7	66	34	0.52	0.41
OCT 6	61	39	0.51	0.50		NOV 8	54	46	0.96	0.34
OCT 7	41	59	0.76	0.57		NOV 9	33	67	0.40	0.33
OCT 8	45	55	0.43	0.55		NOV 10	46	54	0.31	0.55
OCT 9	63	37	0.64	0.44		NOV 11	45	55	0.60	0.76
OCT 10	50	50	0.43	0.40		NOV 12	41	59	0.88	0.51
OCT 11	54	46	0.24	1.15		NOV 13	41	59	0.42	0.61
OCT 12	58	42	0.54	0.55		NOV 14	41	59	0.56	0.62
OCT 13	83 ▶	17	0.27	1.02		NOV 15	50	50	0.55	0.70
OCT 14	33	67	0.07	0.84		NOV 16	41	59	0.25	0.44
OCT 15	33	67	0.56	0.46		NOV 17	61	39	0.58	0.45
OCT 16	58	42	0.35	0.22		NOV 18	41	59	0.39	0.36
OCT 17	58	42	0.64	0.64		NOV 19	41	59	0.51	0.43
OCT 18	58	42	0.38	0.56		NOV 20	58	42	0.81	0.61
OCT 19	33	67	0.57	0.75						
OCT 20	38	62	0.23	0.50						
OCT 21	58	42	0.61	0.49						
OCT 22	45	55	0.39	0.49						
OCT 23	41	59	0.23	0.65						
OCT 24	50	50	0.38	0.58						

SEASONAL FUTURES SPREADS

The commodity spread or straddle was described in Chapter 1. In addition to the use of a technical analytical approach, spreads can be studied on the basis of seasonal tendencies. Some seasonal tendencies have been demonstrated to be highly predictable. It should be understood, however, that spreads are also affected by fundamental conditions such as government programs, weather, supply, demand, interest rates, and carrying charges.

A seasonal spread tendency can be calculated in a fashion very similar to the weekly seasonal price tendency, however one uses the three-weekly spread differences as opposed to the week-to-week futures contract differences. A composite seasonal spread chart showing one of the most repetitive seasonal spreads—long June cattle/short October cattle is shown in Figure 6–8.

Ideally, a speculator would enter long June cattle/short October cattle, buying October cattle, as shown on the chart. Since the start of trading in the live cattle futures contract at the Chicago Mercantile Exchange, this spread has shown a seasonal movement favoring June, during the time period indicated, a great majority of the time. Some other reliable seasonal spreads are shown in Figures 6–9, 6–10, 6–11, and 6–12.

There are several good techniques for seasonal trading that are not only simple to implement, but that can also yield very good results. The seasonal futures methods and the seasonal futures spread methods have good potential for novice traders, since they tend to keep you on the right side of the markets and since they help you trade in the direction of historically valid seasonals. Here, then, are some rules to observe in implementing seasonal trades.

1. **Weekly Seasonal Trading:** Simple Use of Weekly Seasonal Tendencies.

    a. Isolate weekly seasonal tendencies which have high percentage of tendencies toward up or down moves (i.e., 75 percent or more).
    b. Enter position on the last trading day of the week prior to which the seasonal up or down move is likely to occur.

FIGURE 6–8
SEASONAL SPREAD TENDENCY:
JUNE VERSUS OCTOBER LIVE CATTLE

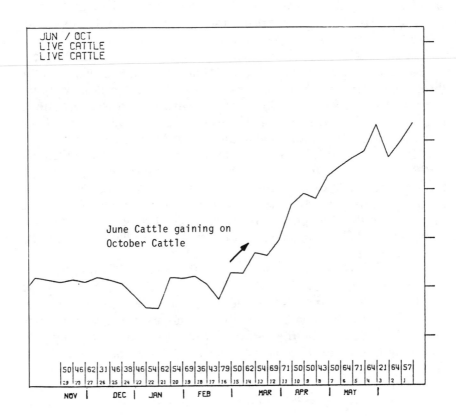

FIGURE 6–9
SEASONAL SPREAD TENDENCY:
JULY VERSUS DECEMBER SOYBEAN MEAL

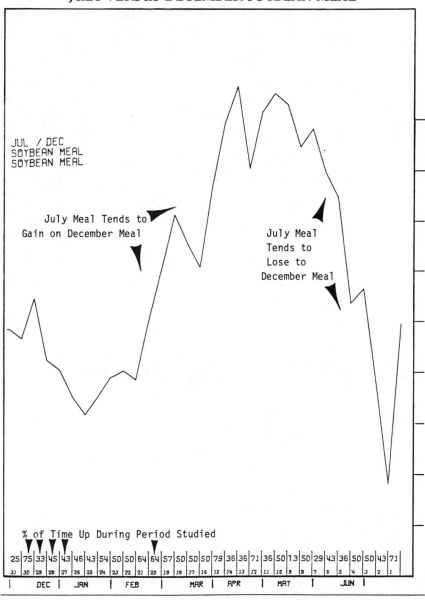

JUL / DEC
SOYBEAN MEAL
SOYBEAN MEAL

July Meal Tends to
Gain on December Meal

July Meal
Tends to
Lose to
December Meal

% of Time Up During Period Studied

| 25 | 75 | 33 | 45 | 43 | 46 | 43 | 54 | 50 | 50 | 64 | 64 | 57 | 50 | 50 | 50 | 79 | 36 | 36 | 71 | 36 | 50 | 13 | 50 | 29 | 43 | 36 | 50 | 50 | 43 | 71 |
| 31 | 30 | 29 | 28 | 27 | 26 | 25 | 24 | 23 | 22 | 21 | 20 | 19 | 18 | 17 | 16 | 15 | 14 | 13 | 12 | 11 | 10 | 9 | 8 | 7 | 6 | 5 | 4 | 3 | 2 | 1 |

| DEC | JAN | FEB | MAR | APR | MAY | JUN |

FIGURE 6–10
SEASONAL SPREAD TENDENCY:
JULY VERSUS OCTOBER COTTON

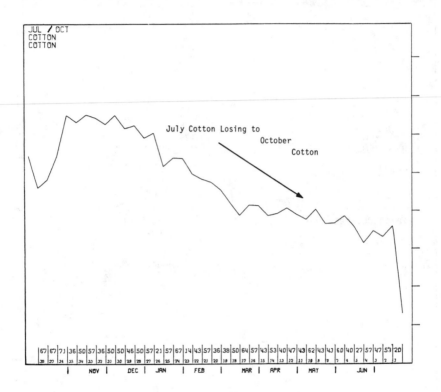

FIGURE 6-11   SEASONAL SPREAD TENDENCY—JULY VERSUS SEPTEMBER COPPER

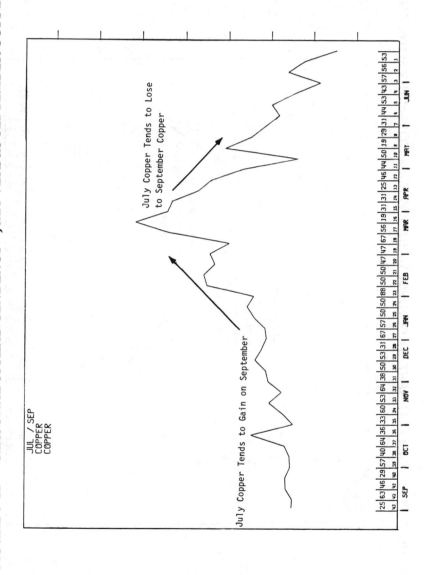

FIGURE 6-12   SEASONAL SPREAD TENDENCY—JULY VERSUS NOVEMBER SOYBEANS

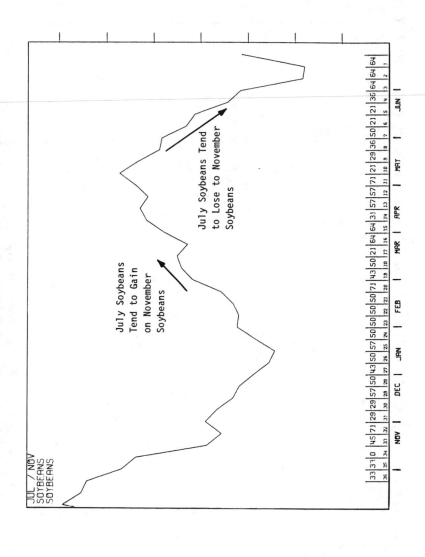

FIGURE 6–13
WEEKLY SEASONAL TENDENCIES USED FOR
SHORT-TERM TRADING ON CURRENT CONTRACT

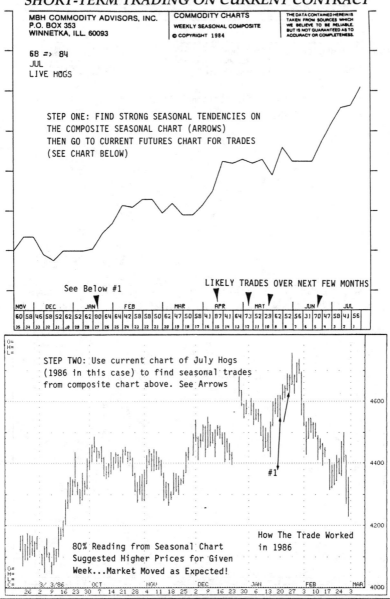

FIGURE 6–14
WEEKLY SEASONAL TENDENCIES USED FOR
SHORT-TERM TRADING ON CURRENT CONTRACT

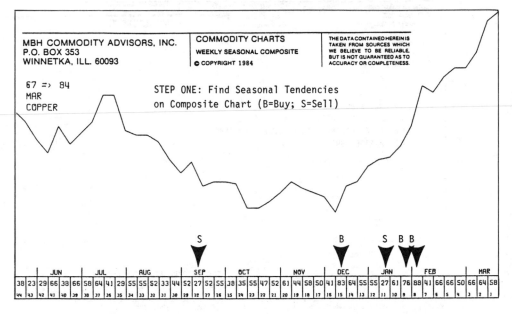

MBH COMMODITY ADVISORS, INC.
P.O. BOX 353
WINNETKA, ILL. 60093

COMMODITY CHARTS
WEEKLY SEASONAL COMPOSITE
© COPYRIGHT 1984

THE DATA CONTAINED HEREIN IS
TAKEN FROM SOURCES WHICH
WE BELIEVE TO BE RELIABLE,
BUT IS NOT GUARANTEED AS TO
ACCURACY OR COMPLETENESS.

67 => 84
MAR
COPPER

STEP ONE: Find Seasonal Tendencies
on Composite Chart (B=Buy; S=Sell)

FIGURE 6–15
WEEKLY SEASONAL TENDENCIES USED FOR
SHORT-TERM TRADING ON CURRENT CONTRACT

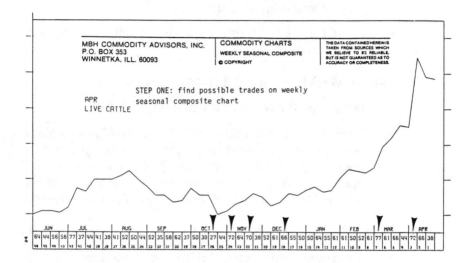

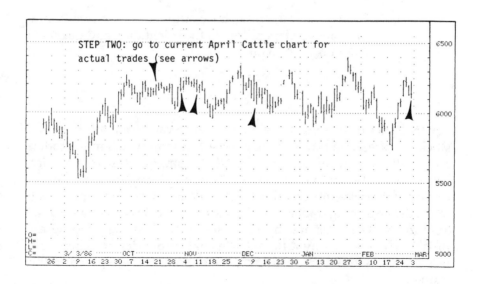

c. Exit the trade during the last trading day of the week of the seasonal move.

d. Alternatively, determine a profit objective based on support or resistance for the current price chart of the given commodity and month.

e. Figures 6–13, 6–14, and 6–15 give specific examples of this approach.

2. **Filtered Weekly Seasonal Trading**

a. Determine the trend of the market.

b. If trend is up, then follow only those weekly percentage readings that are up for the given market and implement steps outlined in Item 1. Do the reverse for markets in downtrends. Specifically, take only those seasonal trades with high percentages on the downside.

3. **Seasonal Spread Trading**

a. Determine which seasonal spread tendencies are reliable.

b. Follow the same procedure outlined for the two techniques above, depending on the orientation and degree of risk you wish to take.

SUMMARY

The existence of seasonal price tendencies in cash commodity prices, stocks, futures, and futures spreads is a fact with which most traders are familiar. However, in spite of modern computer research studies, few traders are well-versed in this important approach to futures trading. Given the historical reliability of many seasonal price patterns, the beginning trader can take considerably less risk by learning how to use seasonals and by using them in his or her trading approach. There are many different seasonal tendencies and many different ways with which to employ them. Some are discussed in this chapter.

Inasmuch as seasonal data is relatively simple to obtain and relatively simple to evaluate, the value of seasonality in most trading approaches is significant. Yet, in spite of the high reliability of some seasonal price tendencies, many systems and traders still buck the trend, refusing to acknowledge the importance of repetitive seasonal patterns in futures prices. I would go so far as to say that seasonality can be used as a good initial indicator for some systems which, when combined with even the most elementary timing indicators, can yield very good results. I encourage more traders to look in the direction of seasonality for potentially valuable trading methods and ideas.

Chapter

7

What You Need to Know about Trading Systems

Since the early 1960s, a variety of trading systems and methods have been introduced to the public. With the rapid growth of professionally managed money and multimillion dollar futures funds, a proliferation of trading systems emerged, many of which made bold promises of profits and success. Claims were often undocumented or poorly researched as historical testing was, for many years, a tedious manual process. The capacity to more readily verify the claims of systems developers increased with the advent of advanced computer testing in the 1980s.

Today, virtually any system can be quickly back-tested by computer, provided its algorithms and money management rules can be programmed. Fraudulent or erroneous claims can be debunked. If a system can be expressed in operational (i.e., programmable) terms, then it can be tested by computer. Virtually any system can be tested and optimized using the computer to test a variety of if-then scenarios.

In this age of computerized everything, virtually every aspect of our lives is, in one way or another, regulated, dominated, determined, or otherwise affected by computers. While some have hailed computers as the solution to all problems, their value is not entirely a *fait accompli*. Alan Watts, venerable American Zen philosopher, rightfully questioned the value of what we call "progress" by noting in his classic, *The Book on the Taboo Against Knowing Who You Are*, that progress is illusory in that most progress is achieved at the expense of other valuable resources. He observed that the very tools which were designed to give us freedom now limit our ability to achieve freedom. We are slaves to computers; we are enslaved by cars and telephones. The technology that was created in order to free us has created so much pollution that we cannot use many of our natural resources without fear of contamination. Have you been at your local forest preserve lately? The signs read "no swimming, no fishing, no skating." They have preserved everything but our right to use them. When computers are out of commission everything seems to come to a stop. And only then do we realize how totally dependent we've become on them.

But the situation is potentially much more serious than its limits on our freedom; computer crime has now definitely become a major concern. It is a sad but true fact that the snake oil salesman of yesteryear has become the computerized trading system salesman of today. One would imagine that the use of a computer would eliminate all doubt about the efficacy of trading systems. If that's what you think then you're dead wrong and it may cost you big bucks before you know you're wrong. The fact of the matter is that computers merely allow shrewd and deceptive con artists to do their work faster, better, and with what appears to be greater credibility. Hiding behind the guise of a bigger, faster, and better computer, these slick operators can develop systems which are without any merit whatsoever, and sell them to an unsuspecting public for big dollars. I call this phenomenon the "P. T. Barnum trading system" effect. Let's examine a few of the common misconceptions and fallacies now prevalent in the field of computerized trading systems and used by system pirates to enhance wrongfully the appearance of their programs.

THE VAST HISTORICAL DATA BASE

Some trading systems assert their superiority based on a vast historical data base. The claim is meaningless. It's a tease, a smoke screen designed to distract attention from the real issues. A lengthy historical data base in and of itself is meaningless. A vast historical data base is only meaningful if it is used appropriately. Unfortunately, most trading system developers use historical data to find the best system fit. They test and retest indicators, add to them, modify them, add rules, change rules, and combine rules until they have found a system that fits the back data perfectly. Once the system is ready, it can be marketed to the public using the lengthy history as a promotional tool. What has the system developer created? Has anything of potential value been found? Odds are slim that anything of substance has been developed. I've found there is an inverse relationship between the complexity of a trading system and its future profitability: The simpler they work, the better they are. If you can find a few simple tools and test them under the appropriate conditions, then they'll continue to work well for you.

THE SELECTIVE DATA-SELECTIVE MARKET TRICK

Another effective trick used by system developers is the limited historical test. By testing a system in trending markets you can create fabulous historical results. And by testing systems for certain markets only, you can show tremendous historical results. Virtually any trading system, no matter how intrinsically flawed, will work in trending markets. Trends make systems right and sideways markets make systems wrong. That's the way it has always been. Some markets are known for their "trendiness"—they establish long-lasting trends and, therefore, show good historical results. Almost any system that follows trends will work in these markets. You don't need a $2,000 software program to make money with them. The best trend-following markets for the last 25 years have been coffee, Yen, cotton, lumber, silver, platinum, Eurodollars, T-Bills, T-Bonds, and the British Pound. Other markets have had good trends, but these markets test best. In some of these markets, simple moving averages have been the best indicators. Be careful of systems designed exclusively for these markets.

WHAT'S THE DRAWDOWN?

Many traders are losers because they quit too soon. The urge to quit is greatest when things are worst. And when things are the worst is when the worst is almost over. But it takes great discipline to persist when all appears lost. When it comes to trading systems, there are two variables that will destroy persistence and discipline—drawdown and consecutive losses. Some systems can produce ten or more consecutive losing trades. And that's enough to test the patience of any trader. But more than the number of consecutive losses is the aggregate dollar amount of those losses. And of even greater importance is the maximum drawdown.

Too many traders ignore drawdown and, therefore, fall victim to its destructive power. Simply stated, maximum drawdown is the maximum decrease in account equity prior to a positive turn in equity. Say, for example, you were ahead $25,000 on your system and that you suffered a $3,000 loss on one trade. If the next trade is also a loser, say $1,200, then the drawdown now is $4,200. And if the next trade is a $400 loser then your drawdown is now $4,600. If the next trade is a winner then this drawdown period ends at $4,600. A new drawdown calculation begins when the next loss is taken.

A drawdown of $1,000 in a $10,000 account is not unreasonable. However, a $1,000 drawdown in a $2,000 account is substantial in terms of percentage. What distinguishes winners from losers many times is the ability to sit through periods of drawdown and, above all, to avoid initiating a trading system during a period of rising equity inasmuch as one could be starting at a high point. If the historical drawdown has not been large then, of course, one could enter at virtually any time. It is still best, however, to begin in a period of drawdown. Nevertheless, human instinct prompts traders to begin with a new system when things look best, not worst. But systems developers will attract you to their systems when things look best, when performance has been on the upswing.

STABLE VS. UNSTABLE SYSTEMS

Another thing to watch out for is a system that has experienced periods of significant volatility. To a certain extent this is related to drawdown. While the best system you can have is one that has shown slow and steady growth through the years, this is, unfortunately, not what interests most traders. Most traders are attracted to systems that boast hundreds or thousands of percent equity increase, not realizing that to achieve such gains it is necessary to risk a large amount of money. Stable, steady growth is by far superior to unstable and volatile performance—but stability frequently fails to attract attention.

DEALING WITH LIMIT MOVES

Since most trading systems are trend-following systems, their entry signals are triggered after bottoms or tops have been made. On occasion, such bottoms or tops are established after important reports which result in limit up or limit down price moves. At times the limit moves will continue for several consecutive days. Some of the biggest moves in history have occurred on a series of limit moves. When a market is "locked" at the limit up, buying is often impossible since there are no sellers. And locked limit down moves afford little or no opportunity to exit a long position, or to enter a short position. Most systems incorrectly assume, in their back testing, that entry was made on limit days when, in fact, entry would *not* have been possible. This allows them to show very large profits on such trades when, in actuality, such trades would have been impossible. Unless a testing program is designed to test for such cases, the hypothetical performance results you'll get are erroneous and misleading. Always inquire as to how locked limit moves were treated in the test and ask for documentation.

CAVEAT EMPTOR

"Let the buyer beware." As computerized trading systems become more and more popular, there will be more and more snake oil salesmen with bigger and better trading systems. The pitfalls are many;

the rewards are few and far between. As a point of information, I always test systems on a "worst case" basis and I suggest you do the same. I design trading systems to reflect the way traders really trade, the way markets really move, and without optimum performance results. The natural order of the markets is entropic. In other words, markets and systems are rarely at their best, often at their worst, and frequently decay over time.

While systems, methods, techniques, computers, and software can provide us with helpful clues about anticipating how markets will behave in the future, there is no guarantee that trading systems will insure success. Many traders erroneously assume an automated trading system will guarantee profitable results. While trading systems are void of emotion and judgment, human beings are not. Ultimately the trade will guide the system to profit or ruin. It is every trader's dream to sit back and let the "dazzling" modern computer go to work generating profitable trades, but humans beings are meddling creatures and will usually attempt to outguess their trading system. It is important, therefore, to see how trading systems interact both with the markets and with the traders who use them.

PROS AND CONS OF TRADING SYSTEMS

Pros

Trading systems facilitate trader discipline. Computerized systems offer additional advantages. The speed and efficiency with which a computer identifies patterns and generates signals is one obvious advantage. Computers can quickly achieve the "number crunching" necessary to recognize trading signals. However, it is impossible for a trader to calculate these signals manually (in the time required), and the trader's ability to evaluate a complete rule-based system is limited as well. Computer systems offer direction and suggestions about what to do in a given market and help limit the range of choices. This makes the trader's task less overwhelming, because the possibilities and opportunities become more clearly defined.

Trading systems approach the market consistently and objectively. Programs are designed logically. Rules are uniformly applied to defined market conditions. Trading systems are effective since rules are not the victims of trader judgment. The whimsical nature of a trader is diminished by a system.

The emotional aspect of trading can be significantly reduced as well since systems are void of emotion and judgment. Unfortunately, the emotional tendency of a trader is to outguess the system—even when it is producing profitable trades! If a trader can discipline himself or herself to follow a system with rigor, emotions will not rule the decision-making process. Trading systems are designed to "think," not to feel.

Another positive feature of trading systems is that they generally include money management rules which facilitate trading discipline.

Cons

One of the more frequent arguments against trading systems is that they can become popular enough to influence the underlying price. This concern has been voiced both by the futures market federal regulatory agency (CFTC) and by individual traders. The concern is that the similarity of computer-based systems used to manage large positions may cause large traders to respond in the same way at the same time, thereby causing distortion in the markets. While it is possible that two systems with the same philosophy may react in similar ways, the chances of precisely similar signals occuring on the same day, at the same time, on the same side of the market, are minimal.

Another argument against trading systems is that markets are random and therefore cannot be based on pattern recognition This argument supports the idea that trading systems based on historical data cannot be valid. While it is not guaranteed that past price patterns guarantee future price patterns, it is also not true that markets are random.

One final argument against the use of trading systems is they define market behavior in limited ways when the market can, in fact, behave in an infinite number of ways. It is believed that because systems are mathematically or mechanically defined, this reduces relationships of events to percentage odds of what could happen next. While the criticism is valid in that systems do capture a very limited number of possibilities, this characteristic is also what makes systems useful. The ability to reduce information to observable patterns gives the trader some semblance of order and direction. Without this, many traders feel overwhelmed and directionless.

Trading systems give the trader a way to interpret, quantify, and classify market behavior. Since trading systems define potential opportunity and provide specific trading signals, following these signals can facilitate the development of trading skills as well as discipline.

OPTIMIZED TRADING SYSTEMS

One of the more controversial techniques to develop as an outgrowth of computerization is the concept of optimization. Optimization is a process by which data is repeatedly tested to find the best results. The best moving average size, point and figure method, or other parameters are made to fit the raw data. Optimization models focus on historical results as predictive of future performance. They assume that risk and reward patterns will not change appreciably over time. This, however, may not be the case, and it is for this reason that commodity trading advisors and money managers must, by law, state, "Past performance does not necessarily imply future success." The caveat should be taken seriously. There have been some sad but true examples of optimized trading systems which perform well based on hypothetical past performance, but which failed miserably when applied in real time.

It is not unusual for the results of an optimized system to appear flawless. Overall past performance looks very profitable, equity drops may appear to be small, and the overall strategy seems to adapt to changing market conditions. And yet, the real-time application of the system will often prove to have less than desirable results.

It is important, therefore to use a system with predictive qualities rather than one which is historically fitted. Questions to ask about all systems are:

1. Does the system have face validity? Does it make sense?

2. Can the system adjust to changing market conditions in real time?

3. Does the system have too many variables? The more variables it has, the less successful it will be in the future.

Although these three points are important, there are other performance criteria that can be used to evaluate any trading strategy during the test phase or under actual market time. One significant factor to be reviewed is the consistency of the trading strategy over a long period of time. Stability over time is critical. Be sure the test data is long enough to include changes in price level. Bull and bear markets should be covered as well as periods of extended low volatility.

It is important to understand the methods of optimization and to provide proper precautions regarding optimized trading systems. Performed properly, extensive testing can reveal a great deal. However, excessive optimizing can be misleading, deceptive, and costly.

GUIDELINES FOR SELECTING EFFECTIVE TRADING SYSTEMS

Anyone who has been involved in futures trading, even if for a short period of time, has undoubtedly heard claims that the "perfect system" has been developed. The dream of sitting back and letting a computer system do all of the work is enticing but illusory. There are many traders who have traded systems without doing the necessary homework, and have learned about systems the costly way. Having a framework with which to ask the right questions is an important part of selecting a trading system. It is to the trader's benefit to do some ground work before rushing in and blindly adopting a new system. Taking into consideration your particular style of trading and your temperament is also helpful and necessary in selecting a trading system.

The performance issues to be considered in evaluating a trading system are:

1. Actual length of the historical test or real time application.

2. Money management philosophy.

3. Trading philosophy.

4. Ratio of net cumulative profit to drawdown.

5. Maximum winning trade.

6. Maximum losing trade.

7. Average profit or loss per trade.

8. Number of consecutive losing trades.

9. Distribution of profits over time.

10. Frequency of trading—systems designed to trade on a short-term basis may not take into account slippage and commission costs which can be high enough to significantly reduce the probability of profits.

There are many different trading systems to choose from and a wide variety of approaches to use in developing a trading system. Beginners are advised to keep things simple and to use a trading system that is programmed with indicators suited to your comfort level. Over time, you can learn to incorporate different indicators into your trading strategy and learn to customize trading models. Be forewarned, however, that more indicators do not necessarily mean a better system. In fact, there is a point of diminishing returns.

Finally, it cannot be overemphasized that consistency is the key consideration in any trading system. You are far, far better off with slow and steady growth than with violent equity swings. Following these guidelines and remembering that it is the trader who makes the system succeed or fail will help you achieve your goals as a trader. Any successful approach to trading the futures markets requires common sense, business-like decision-making, and sound risk management as its quintessential elements.

SUMMARY

Computerized trading systems have expanded the scope of futures traders. Systems can now be thoroughly back-tested and perfected using the computer to test many if-then scenarios. Trading systems offer a way to define, quantify, and categorize market behavior by reducing information to patterns and generating trading signals. While systems are void of emotion, traders are not and often try to outguess a system. Misuse and lack of discipline are major causes of losses in trading systems.

Methods of optimized trading systems were explained and precautions regarding the relationship of past performance to future success were emphasized. This chapter provided the pros and cons of trading systems and offered some specific guidelines upon which to evaluate computer systems. I stressed that traders make the system and not vice versa.

Part

2

Discipline and Trading

Chapter

8

Discipline: The First Key to Success

Although there are many things I could tell you about different trading approaches and the lessons I have learned through long and hard experience, none of them would be more meaningful than the lessons I have learned about discipline. The advice I can give you about this single most important area of success in futures trading is the most important knowledge I can impart. If I were to suggest that you read only one chapter in this book, this would be it!

When asked what is the single most important variable to success in futures trading, my response is not "trading systems," nor is it "the type of computer you have," nor is it "the type of inside information to which you might be privy." It is not "the amount of capital you have," or "the broker with whom you are trading." What does ultimately separate winners from losers, commercial, speculative, short-term, long-term, or otherwise, is discipline in its many facets.

To most traders discipline is just another well-worn topic in futures trading. They have heard the word, they've studied the preaching, and they believe they have learned the lessons. My observations and experiences with futures markets and futures traders leads me to the irreversible conclusion that the lessons have not been learned!

The word discipline signifies something traders know they need and believe they have. In their heart of hearts, however, most traders know they are sorely lacking in discipline, and that they will probably never have it.

Discipline is virtually impossible to teach or to learn from anyone else. It is complex, elusive, evasive, and often camouflaged. It is the *sine qua non* of success in virtually every form of human achievement, in every field, and in every generation. Yet, to the best of my knowledge there is no simple way to define discipline.

There are futures traders who have virtually no objective trading system to speak of, but who, through the application and development of discipline, have achieved success. On the other hand, there are many futures traders with excellent trading systems, who for lack of discipline have remained unsuccessful, in spite of massive statistical evidence to suggest their techniques are indeed valid and capable of producing tremendous profits.

Discipline can transform a marginal trading system into a highly successful one. Lack of discipline can transform a potentially successful trading system into a consistent and persistent losing approach. In reviewing the history, literature, and facts about virtually any form of investing or speculating, I have found that a key element of success is discipline.

The purpose of this chapter is twofold: first to underscore the importance of discipline; and second, to suggest a number of ways by which discipline can be developed and improved. First, let's look at the fashion in which discipline functions, and at its ramifications in the successful trading approach.

WHY DISCIPLINE IS IMPORTANT

As you know, there are many different approaches to futures trading. Some are potentially more profitable than others. Some are simple, some are complex, some are logical, and some not so logical. Regardless of the trading approach one employs, all trading systems and methods have certain elements in common. These are:

1. Specific signals (rules) for entry and exit.

2. Specific parameters, methods of calculation of timing signals.

3. Specific action that must be taken as a function of 1 and 2.

When systems and methods are tested by computer in order to generate hypothetical or ideal results, they are not tested in real time, but rather in theoretical time, with perfect adherence to the trading rules that have been programmed into the computer. What gets tested is a series of specific parameters. What comes out is a listing of trades and hypothetical results based on the perfect execution of the rules that were programmed into the machine.

The output of the system test will yield many different types of information including such things as percentage of trades profitable, percentage of trades unprofitable, percentage of trades that break even, average winning trade in dollars, average losing trade in dollars, performance for given markets, average length of time per trade. All data derived from the computer test of a trading model is based upon perfect follow-up, implementation, and execution of trading signals according to the parameters programmed into the computer. There is no room for error!

There is no room for lack of discipline! Some systems are profitable only 55–65 percent of the time. Other systems show higher percentages. But such statistics can be misleading. I have rarely seen systems that are profitable more than 80 percent of the time. Certainly you can imagine that a trading system which is correct 90 percent of the time, making a $100 profit on the average each time and then losing $900 on the occasion that it is wrong, would certainly not be very profitable. Furthermore, the individual trading the system would give back all profits made on nine trades on one losing trade! One losing trade would bring the account back to even. Should there be another error due to lack of discipline, the account would show a net loss.

Conversely, a trading system may show eight losers for every two winners. If, however, the average profitable trade is much larger than the average losing trade, even a system having nine losers out of every 10 trades could be profitable, if the bottom line per trade were higher on the winning side. Nevertheless, such a system would be thrown astray if lack of discipline resulted in much larger losses than expected for the eight losing trades. If lack of discipline interfered significantly with the profits on the two profitable trades, then the net results might be much worse than anticipated.

A third scenario would be a marginal trading system. Assume a trading system is profitable about 65 percent of the time. In such cases, we can figure that approximately 65 out of every 100 trades are winners, and 35 are losers. You can see that only 30 percent separates the winners from the losers. In other words, the trader must have sufficient discipline to keep the losses as small as possible, and to maximize profits. This is where discipline enters into the formula.

Discipline is the machinery that can make or break any trading system. There are some conditions under which discipline will not be the important variable. However, in most cases it is the significant variable. All the glowing trading statistics for your trading system will be totally useless if you are not capable of duplicating the exact statistics generated by the computer test of your trading system. In other words, you must stick as close to the averages as possible or one or two losses much larger than the average, or one or two profits much smaller than the average, will be sufficient to ruin your results. Sometimes this can occur strictly as a function of market behavior (i.e., limit moves against you). However, more often than not, as I have stated before, it is the trader who is responsible for maintaining the discipline of a system.

DOING YOUR "HOMEWORK"

It is uncanny how many times markets will begin major moves in line with the expectations of many advisors, analysts, and speculators without these various individuals being on board for the big move. Why do things like this happen? How often has this happened to you? I know from personal experience that many individuals have good records at predicting where prices will go. I also know that when it comes to doing their homework, they have especially poor records.

What do I mean by doing homework? I mean very simply, keeping up to date on the signals generated by the system or systems you are following. In order to keep in touch with the markets according to your system, you will need to have a regular schedule for doing the technical or fundamental work your system requires. Whether this consists of simple charting that may take only five minutes per day, or complex mathematical calculations that may take considerably longer, the fact remains that the discipline of doing your homework is one of the prerequisites for successful trading.

If you have a system and do not follow it, you are guilty of poor discipline. If you have a system and fail to do the work which generates your trading signals, then you are just as guilty of lacking discipline. As you can see, and as you can well appreciate, it is a sad but true fact that most traders don't even get past the first step.

Can you identify strongly, or even partially with some of the things I am saying? How often have you been in the situation of missing a move because your charts or systems were not up to date? How many times has this frustrated you into making an unwarranted decision in an effort to compensate for your first error? If the truth were fully known, we would know that many of us are guilty. The sad fact about this situation is that its rectification is a very simple matter. In fact, the steps one must take in order to rectify virtually any problem resulting from lack of trading discipline are very specific, easily understood, and exceptionally elementary to implement.

It is unfortunately true that the discipline required to trade consistently and successfully is the same type of discipline required in virtually every aspect of human life. Whether it is the discipline required to lose weight, stop smoking, or develop a successful business, the basics of all discipline are the same.

If you develop discipline in your trading, I am certain that it will spread to other areas of your life, including your personal affairs. Unfortunately, however, discipline in other aspects of your life may not necessarily spread very quickly to your trading. The nature of futures trading provides serious challenges to discipline developed in other areas of life. Suggestions for improving discipline will be provided later on in this chapter.

HOW LACK OF DISCIPLINE BECOMES CHRONIC

Lack of discipline is not confined to any one situation, any one trade, or any one trader. Lack of discipline is a way of life, albeit a bad one. Individuals who achieve success without adhering to certain disciplined practices do so as a stroke of good fortune, and stand the chance of forfeiting their wealth through a lack of disciplined action. Unfortunately, lack of discipline is not a simple matter, but rather it spreads like a cancerous growth through the trader's behavior. This should come as no surprise to those who understand relationships, whether they are those of individuals or those between the individual and the marketplace. In an interpersonal relationship, lack of discipline and specificity can cause negative interaction. Negative interaction will then result in further tests of discipline and self-control. These will, in turn, result in other problems—failures and negative experiences—until the entire relationship is threatened. The same is true of one's trading.

Lack of discipline in instituting a trade may frustrate the trader into a further display of poor discipline. After several such incidents the trader will become frustrated, causing further errors to become likely. The net result is usually a succession of errors each compounding upon the other and each likely far worse than the previous. It is for this reason that one must take great care to avoid making even the first mistake due to a lack of discipline. The first mistake will lead to the second, the second may lead to four others, and four others may lead to 16 others. This is the manner in which a lack of discipline tends to spread. Frequently it can grow at an exponential rate.

SUGGESTIONS FOR IMPROVING YOUR DISCIPLINE

I certainly don't have all the answers for improving your discipline. However, I do have a number of very cogent, time-tested techniques to help you improve. All of the suggestions will require action and thorough implementation if they are to have a beneficial effect on your results.

1. **Make a Schedule.**

   In order to help you keep your trading signals up to date, set aside a given time of the day or week during which you will do the necessary calculations, charts, or other market work. Doing the same work every day of the week will help you get into a specific routine, and this in turn, will eliminate the possibility (or greatly reduce it) of not being prepared when a major move develops.

2. **Don't Try to Do Too Much.**

   Attempt to specialize in one particular trading approach. If you try to trade in too many markets at one time, or with too many systems at one time, your work will become a burden, you will not look forward to it, and you will be more prone to let your studies fall behind. Ideally, seek to work in no more than three to five markets at any given time, and attempt to specialize in only one specific system.

3. **Use a Checklist.**

   One of my favorite analogies is the similarity between the trader and the airplane pilot. Before take-off a good airplane pilot goes through his or her pre-flight checklist. I certainly would not want to fly in a plane with a pilot who was sloppy in this procedure—would you?

   The trader who wishes to eliminate trading errors should also maintain such a checklist, consulting it regularly, preferably before each trade is made. Of all of my suggestions the checklist is probably the best one for all traders. I would suggest that even after your checklist has become automatic, you still maintain it, since lack of discipline is likely to attack you at almost any time. It can strike without notice and often does.

4. **Do Not Accept Third-Party Input Once Your Decision Has Been Made.**
    I have come to respect the fact that good traders are usually loners. They must do their work in isolation, and they must implement their decisions in isolation. A pushy or talkative broker, a well-intentioned friend or a very persuasive newsletter can often sway you from a decision that only you should make. There are times when your decision will be wrong, but these are part of the learning experience, and you alone must make your decisions based on the facts as you see them.

    If you have decided to follow your own trading system, then by all means follow it and forget about other input. If, however, your system is based on input from other sources, then try to implement your decisions without being swayed from them once your mind has been made up. The benefits of deciding on your own far outweigh the potential benefits of having too much input.

5. **Evaluate Your Progress**
    Feedback is a very important part of the learning process. Keep track of how you are doing with your trading not only in terms of dollars and cents but in terms of specific signals, behavior, and techniques. This will give you an idea of how closely you are staying with the rules, which rules you are breaking, and how often you may be breaking them.

    It is important to know when you make mistakes, but it is more important to know what kind of mistakes you make and how often you make them. This will help you overcome the lack of discipline that causes trading errors to occur.

6. **Learn from Every Loss.**
    Losses are tuition. They are expensive and they must be good for something. Learn from each loss and do your very best to avoid taking the same loss twice or more for the same

reason. Do not repeat the same errors. To do so indicates that your discipline is not improving.

7. **Understand Yourself.**
    This is certainly a big job and not one easily accomplished. It is extremely important that you understand your motivation and your true reasons for trading the markets. Frequently individuals will do poorly in the markets because their objectives and goals are not well-established. Self-understanding helps clarify your personal goals and thereby makes the process of attaining your goals more specific. I will discuss this issue at greater length in another chapter.

8. **Work with Your Trading System and Remain Dedicated to It.**
    If you are like most traders, you will have done considerable research on a trading method or system. Some traders, however, become quickly disenchanted with their systems and hop from one technique to another. This is one of the worst forms of poor discipline. It does not allow sufficient time for a system to perform. In so doing, the speculator takes considerably more overall risk than he or she should.

9. **Check Your Objectives.**
    At times, poor training discipline can be a function of unclear objectives. If you have decided that you want to trade for the short term only, then you have a very clear objective. However, if you are not certain about the time frame of your trading, about the trading system you plan to use as your vehicle, about the relationship you wish to have with your broker, about the quotation equipment you plan to use (if any), then you will be prone to make mistakes and have poor discipline.

My suggestion is to make all major trading decisions before you even get started with your trading. Some corrections can be made along the way, but a majority of decisions must be made prior to any serious trading.

10. Know When to Quit.
In order to improve your trading discipline, it is important to have an objective measure of when you will terminate a given trade, profitably or unprofitably. Whether this is done at a particular price or a particular dollar amount is of no consequence. The fact remains that you must know when you have had enough.

11. Make Commitments and Keep Them.
In trading it is important to make and keep commitments in the markets just as it is in every phase of human endeavor and interaction. If, however, you do not make a commitment, or if the commitment you make is not clear, then you stand the chance of not following through on an important phase of your trading. For this reason I encourage all traders to make specific commitments, not only in terms of such things as trading systems, trading approach, available capital, maximum risk, but also in terms of each and every trade they make.

Do not make the trade unless you are fully committed to it. What does this mean? It means that many individuals are prone to establish a position in the market based on what "looks like" a good signal or when it "looks like the market wants to turn higher." In other words, commitments are made on the basis of vague indications.

In order to make a commitment that will serve you well, do not make commitments based on sketchy information. The uneasy feeling you get when you make such a decision will be enough to let you know that you are not making a commitment based on correct procedures.

There are many more ways to improve your discipline, but quite a few of these are probably very specific to your individual situation. One good way in which to determine how, where, when, and what type of commitment you wish to make is to examine yourself using a checklist or questionnaire designed to ascertain the precise nature of your situation. Ordinarily, this can be done with only a brief amount of thought and analysis.

SUMMARY

With the possible exception of persistence, discipline is the single most important quality a trader can possess. Though discipline cannot be taught or learned in a classroom setting, there are many things traders can do to facilitate the learning process. This chapter discussed the relevant aspects of discipline and made suggestions regarding how discipline might be improved.

Chapter

9

The Art and Science of Contrary Thinking

Hundreds of years ago, when the tulip mania was sweeping Holland, no one would have envisioned that many years later, the events of those times would be seen as lessons for the speculator of modern times.

The tulip mania was an event that marked a dark but exemplary period in the psychological and economic history of humankind. The mania swept Holland in the 1600s with panic buying of a commodity that was in great demand, but that had no value other than what people were willing to buy and sell it for. The price of tulip bulbs increased by several thousandfold over a brief period of time, during which frenzied speculation engulfed virtually all of Holland. Overnight, fortunes were made and lost as speculators rushed to buy and sell this "precious commodity."

Today we can only look back in wonderment on those times, shaking our heads and saying, "How could something like this have happened?" Yet, we need not look too far back in our own history to see countless examples of similar manias sweeping our markets. Whether these occurred in the areas of land, real estate, precious metals, sugar, or the stock market, is irrelevant. The fact remains that panic and mania are still very much a part of our modern society. Emotion still closely governs speculators in all walks of life and in all markets.

In our troubled and volatile times, there is no single market sector as subject to emotional fluctuations as is the futures market. The slightest rumor or news can send the markets skyrocketing or plummeting precipitously with no seeming end in sight as the frenzy feeds upon itself.

Ultimately, economic reality takes hold and prices eventually return to their proper levels. In the interim, however, emotion and psychology rule the pits. To understand the psychology of the pit, to understand the psychology of the crowd, to understand the psychology of the speculator, and to understand the manner in which these can be best used to your advantage, is to understand the power and the art of contrary opinion.

Although the power of contrary thinking is well-documented and well-understood, it is somewhat unquantifiable, and hence rather elusive in spite of its immense conceptual value. An idea that cannot be quantified is, unfortunately, one that will be difficult to employ in a scientific setting. This is why the concepts advanced by proponents of contrary thinking do not necessarily correspond with the performance of contrary opinion techniques. However, let's first examine precisely what I mean by contrary opinion in order to see how it can be of practical value to the speculator.

WHAT IS IT?

Contrary thinking is the art of thinking and interpreting reality in a different way from the majority of individuals. Contrary thinking is possible in every form of human endeavor and there are literally millions of individuals who are contrary thinkers as a way of life.

Thought, however, does not necessarily lead to action, and I think we should understand at the outset that there is a vast difference between contrary thinkers and contrary doers. More about this later.

Contrary thinkers want to "zig" while everyone else is "zagging." They expect higher prices while most people expect lower prices. They expect lower prices when most people expect higher prices. Contrary thinking is not necessarily a measure of stubbornness, but rather the ability to avoid being caught up in the sentiment of the "crowd."

There are many extremes in the marketplace and it is a matter of record that some people are swayed by the direction of a major trend and, moreover, that they are strongly influenced by the opinions of others. Therefore, market movement in a particular direction, if strong enough and long enough, tends to arouse public interest. Traders and investors develop tunnel vision. They see only what they have been told to see, or only what they want to see.

The important facts, the ones that will lead to an eventual change in trend, are often ignored. Even when markets begin to change direction, those who have been mesmerized into fervently believing that the trend has not ended will continue to cling desperately to their beliefs. In the meantime, the contrary thinker has suspected all along that the direction of the trend was due to change, and that the opportunity for profit lay just around the corner.

CLASSIC EXAMPLES

There are literally hundreds of classic examples in the economic history of the world to support the theory that a strong consensus of opinion often suggests an eventual opposite price movement. I could probably turn this chapter into several by citing some examples of contrary opinion in contemporary times. However, my job is not to function as a history teacher; rather it is to familiarize you with valuable concepts that should be added to your trading repertoire. My comments will therefore be brief. For specific examples please refer to the reading list and the bibliography at the end of this book.

ALL AROUND US

Contrary thinking is valuable not only in the markets, but also in everyday life. There have been many fads and financial fallacies in modern times, but the majority of investors and traders have not learned anything about their own emotional makeup in spite of these events.

The writings of the masters clearly underscore the importance of being a contrarian. To act and think contrary to the crowd is a valuable personal quality in every walk of life. Yet, it is important that the contrary thoughts and actions be selective. It is important that contrariness be employed at crucial turning points in our lives and in the markets.

QUANTIFICATION

There have been a number of attempts throughout the history of the markets to quantify various measures of contrary opinion. These have, however, been only sporadically successful. The concept of odd-lot short sales in the stock market is one application of contrary opinion. It is a measure, essentially, of how bearish small investors are at any given time. Naturally, one would expect on the basis of contrary opinion that the more bearish small investors are, the more likely prices are to continue rising. Odd-lot short sales are a measure of actual short selling by small investors as an expression of their bullish or bearish sentiment.

The explanation of this phenomenon is, of course, very simple. Essentially it says that the small trader cannot afford to sell short a round lot (100 share blocks) of stock. Furthermore, the odd-lotter is felt to be unsophisticated and relatively uninformed. Therefore, a high bearish consensus of action among odd-lot short sellers often indicates that the opposite is about to happen.

Historically, the odd-lot short sales indicator has translated into a very good tool. On occasion, the odd-lot short sellers have been right, but rarely for too long, and rarely for too much of a move. More often than not, they are incorrect at critical turning points in the stock market.

R. E. Hadady has advanced the notion that contrary opinion in the futures markets can be measured quantitatively by conducting a survey of sentiment among brokers and advisors on a weekly basis. His reporting service, Market Vane, reports regularly the percentages of bullish sentiments for each individual futures market. A sample of Hadady's work is shown in Figure 9–1.

The Hadady theory is a most interesting one and its concepts are valid, yet there is still the nagging question about its inability to be more precise in timing the market turns. Hadady has developed a number of techniques for making timing more precise, yet it would seem to me that there must be a better way to employ contrary opinion in the futures markets. My main objection is that most contrary opinion surveys merely reflect opinion and not action, and that there is a large disparity between market opinion and market action. Whereas a market may rise and opinions may continue to become exceptionally bullish, if these bullish opinions are not backed up by extremely persistent buying by the public, then the opinions are not especially valid. Contrary opinion works because opinions lead to action. If there is only contemplation but no action, then opinions may not be so valid.

The techniques developed by Hadady and other followers of contrary opinion have great potential in the markets, but they must be backed up by good timing. If you plan to use bullish consensus or contrary opinion indicators, be certain you use them in conjunction with timing indicators such as those described in this book, or with other traditional but effective tools.

Essentially, a bullish consensus will let you know when the markets have reached a danger zone on the upside, suggesting the possibility of a top or a potential bottom due to exceptionally bearish public and professional sentiment. Figures 9–2, 9–3, and 9–4 illustrate three interesting situations with extreme levels of bullish consensus and timing indicators to suggest a turn in the market. As previously mentioned, the combination of timing and contrary opinion has great potential for all traders. The contrary thinker should always be in touch with levels of bullish or bearish consensus. Though an extreme level on either side does not warrant immediate action, such extremes do suggest that a change in trend could occur very soon.

FIGURE 9–1
BULLISH CONSENSUS IN A SPECIFIC FUTURES CONTRACT
(Hadady, 1983, page C4)

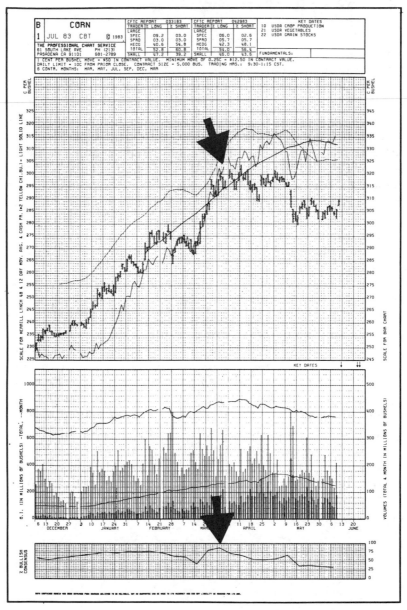

Reprinted with permission of Market Vane, 61 S. Lake Ave., #309 Pasadena, CA 91101

FIGURE 9–2
(Hadady, 1983, page C25)

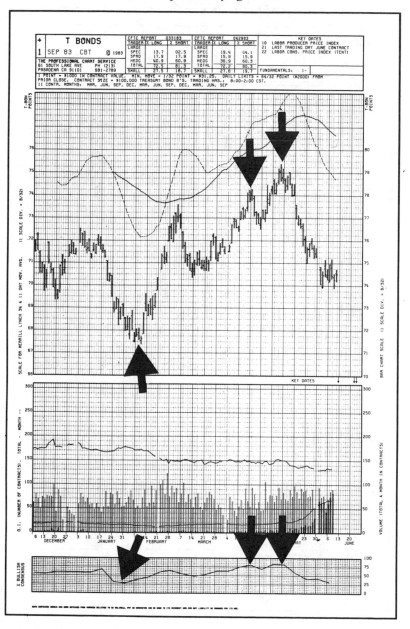

Reprinted with permission of Market Vane, 61 S. Lake Ave., #309 Pasadena, CA 91101

FIGURE 9–3
(Hadady, 1983, page C25)

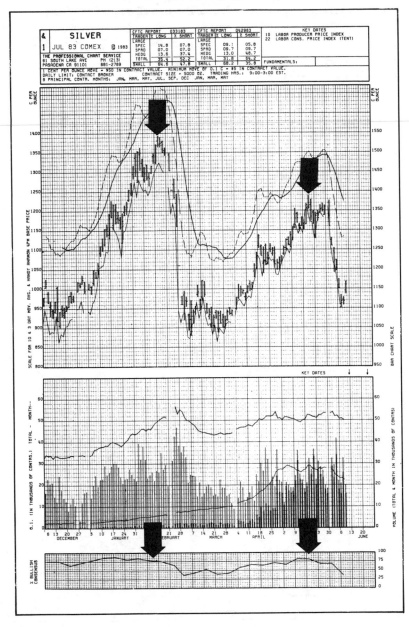

Reprinted with permission of Market Vane, 61 S. Lake Ave., #309 Pasadena, CA
91101

FIGURE 9–4
(Hadady, 1983, page C25)

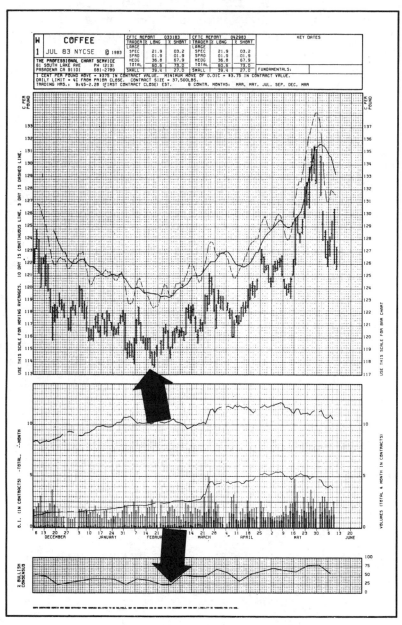

Reprinted with permission of Market Vane, 61 S. Lake Ave., #309 Pasadena, CA 91101

DAILY SENTIMENT INDEX

The Daily Sentiment Index (DSI) is an informational tool I developed based upon ideas of contrary opinion. My staff surveys the opinions of futures traders on a daily basis recording their opinions as either bullish, bearish, or no comment. When compiled, the data reflects the percentage of bullish sentiment by market and provides traders with a timely assessment of market sentiment.

THEORY OF DSI

DSI theory is based on the hypothesis that market sentiment tends to peak and trough with prices. The central aspect of DSI theory is that on any given day a high level of bullish or bearish sentiment, as determined by my survey, will generally indicate an opposite move in the direction of the market. Oftentimes the move will arrive sooner, rather than later. For example, when my survey indicates 80 percent or more bullish sentiment, I likely interpret this as an indication that the market is topping and will likely move lower. On the other hand, if my survey indicates that traders are highly bearish (i.e., 80 percent or more agree a decline will occur), then one should expect prices to move higher.

Contrary opinion is, by definition, an opinion that is opposite to the view held by the majority of market participants. If the majority expects prices to rise, a "contrarian" would be bearish, expecting prices to decline. Many different techniques may be used to detect prevailing market opinions. There are different ways to gather the data as well. Central to any contrary opinion methodology is the idea that strong agreement that anticipates market direction generally indicates that price trend is likely to turn in the direction opposite the consensus.

GUIDELINES FOR USING DSI

In order to make effective use of DSI, here are suggestions to follow:

1. Keep track of the percentages daily for several weeks.

2. Be aware, by recording daily, the high (80 percent and over) and low (20 percent and under) percentages.

3. Observe price behavior on the following day and for several days thereafter.

4. Watch for price moves that are opposite from the extreme sentiment readings (i.e., when DSI is 80 percent or over, watch for prices to move lower). If DSI is 20 percent or under, expect prices to move higher.

5. Look for many days of extreme sentiment readings in relation to significant tops or bottoms.

6. Develop your own method of application. I suggest using technical timing indicators to trigger market entry when sentiment is extreme.

DSI and other contrary opinion systems do not guarantee success in trading futures markets. DSI is a tool for interpreting "overbought" and "oversold" market conditions. When used in conjunction with other indicators and your own timing techniques, DSI application can help you anticipate potential changes in market trend. It can also serve as a warning signal that will help you avoid buying tops and selling bottoms.

COMMITMENT OF TRADERS REPORT

Another way to determine the bullish or bearish attitudes of the traders is by studying the monthly *CFTC Commitment of Traders Report*. This report contains valuable information on the composition of longs and shorts in the marketplace by percentages and groups, showing increases and/or decreases from previous monthly levels. Unfortunately, the report is monthly, and by the time the news is available to most traders it is likely that a change in the numbers has already occurred. If these figures could be obtained weekly, they would be an invaluable source of information to all speculators.

For those who are seriously interested in studying contrary opinion and bullish consensus relationships in the markets, this type of information is essential. The individual or organization who can develop a reporting system that studies similar distribution or that arrives at the heart of bullish/bearish consensus in a more specific and, in particular, more frequent fashion, will truly have an exceptionally valuable market tool.

SUMMARY

Contrary opinion is an important market concept. It allows you to develop an opinion that is often opposite from the view held by the majority of market participants. Traders should monitor the consensus of bullish opinion, taking caution when levels become too high or too low. In this chapter, I discussed the disparity between market opinion and market action. The Daily Sentiment Index was introduced and specific guidelines for applying DSI were illustrated.

Chapter

10

How to Trade Like a Pro

During my years as a futures trader, I have seen many investors prosper, but many more fail. What separates a winner from a loser is not, at first, easily discernable. In the business of trading, we measure success in terms of money. However, defining the actual behavior of a winner is considerably more elusive.

I have found that the attitudes and behaviors of a winner are markedly different from those of a loser. A winner will be flexible in his or her thinking, admit to being wrong, and be willing to learn from mistakes. A loser, on the other hand, often sabotages his or her own trading with self-defeating attitudes, stubborn beliefs, and an unwillingness to learn.

My work has shown that futures trading is similar to most other businesses. Whether a person is involved in sports, medicine, sales, or trading, the attitudes and behaviors will determine the degree of success which can be achieved. True, there are some clear-cut differences between trading and other fields. However, there are more similarities than there are differences. Let's take a look at some of the common traits shared by most successful individuals, regardless of their specific profession or vocation. Here are some characteristics revealed by my observations and experience.

1. Discipline is an absolute necessity. Whether you're a football quarterback, a retail salesperson, or futures account manager, you must learn how to manage your emotions and be mentally fit to be successful at any game. Learning to be in control of your emotions will enable you to be more objective in any environment where you choose to participate. Being objective will enhance your capacity to recognize an opportunity and will help you to know when not to take action. Oftentimes, traders feel they must always be involved in the market. Knowing when to stay out is as important as knowing when to take advantage of an opportunity. This requires self-control, discipline, and the ability to act on opportunities at the right time. Discipline is also required in attending to day-to-day details of your business. If trading is your business, then the day-to-day operations must necessarily include your chart work, calculations, system evaluation signals, and bookkeeping. For more details on discipline, see Chapter 8.

2. Persistence is second on my list, but it ranks equally in importance with discipline. In every form of business, persistence pays off. Persistence means you hang in even if you have experienced rejection or defeat. A successful salesperson does not give up if he or she experiences a dry spell when no one is buying. Similarly, a good trader does not take a string of losses personally. A good trader will attempt to learn from prior mistakes and persist in developing winning trades. There is, however, a fine line between persistence and bull-headedness. In futures trading, as in other businesses, it may take quite a few successive losses before a large victory can be attained. Although it is important to learn from mistakes and admit when you are wrong, it is also important to know when not to quit. Persistence is also vital in finding a trading system or method that is best suited to your needs.

3. Patience is an important quality. It is often necessary to wait for the right opportunities, rather than acting on the wrong ones. Since there are many incorrect actions one can take in the market, it is important to wait for the right opportunities. Many traders are anxious and fear they are missing something if they are not always participating in the market. The patient trader has confidence in waiting for the correct opportunity to present itself.

4. Independence is an important characteristic. Learning to think on our own is not something we are taught in school. However, most successful people in any business have taught themselves independent thinking. This often requires going against the norm and establishing a perspective that is different from the crowd. This can be uncomfortable for many people. As a trader, it is often necessary to ignore well-intentioned input from friends, associates, and brokers. Trading ideas, trading systems, and implementation of trades involves singleness of purpose and firm resolution. Therefore, it is necessary for a successful trader to develop independent thinking and avoid the "herd" mentality.

5. Contrary thinking is, perhaps, the single most significant psychological quality a trader can possess. If contrary thinking is not one of your traits, you must work toward developing it. A common quandary of most traders is the fear of going against the crowd. Cultivating the art of contrary thinking allows a trader to take actions that oppose the majority. This is important, as generally the majority is wrong and public losses are commonplace. It is crucial, therefore, to learn how to assess what the crowd is thinking and develop the courage to take an independent trading approach in the market. Contrary opinion will also help the trader avoid being trapped when the public takes hold of a market and panics. An astute trader can take advantage of the emotional extremes in the market and step in when severe moves are about over, taking appropriate positions accordingly.

6. Honesty with yourself is important and requires you to make a rigorous assessment of your strengths and weaknesses. This is not often easy and it is seldom done. Human beings are more inclined to blame other people and situations for their failures in life. Assuming total responsibility for your actions is a difficult task, but is absolutely required for achieving success as a trader, or in other business endeavors. Developing the skills of responsibility demands a hard and honest look at where you are competent, and where you are incompetent. One thing is sure: the market will show you! Therefore, it is in your best interest to engage in a continuous process of self-reflection. Learning to take an honest inventory of yourself will enable you to accentuate your strengths and work on the weaknesses that make you vulnerable in the market.

7. The ability to act quickly, though last on my list of the top seven qualities, is by no means last in importance. There is a clear and important distinction between developing a sense of urgency and acting impulsively. A good trader wants to constantly pay attention and be ready to take action without being too spontaneous or whimsical. As you've seen in previous chapters, the futures markets are fast. They do not wait. A trader cannot feel overwhelmed by indecision and fear. This will foster a sense of paralysis, where no action will be taken. It is not enough just to be in the right place at the right time. You must also act. There are ways in which this skill can be developed, and if you do not possess this quality now, you will need to learn the perceptual tools to improve your capacity to act.

To impress upon you the importance of how quickly the futures markets move, examine Figure 10–1. This figure shows December silver futures prices on a 15-minute bar chart of the high, low, open and close during the period 10/19/84 through 10/26/84. Examine very carefully the behavior of prices on 10/25. Note that during this particular day the price of December silver futures moved from a low of 731 up to a daily high of 755 (a move of $1,700 per contract) during

FIGURE 10-1 FIFTEEN-MINUTE DECEMBER SILVER FUTURES CHART
SHOWING LARGE INTRADAY MOVE IN PRICE
(Reprinted with Permission of Commodity Quote Graphics)

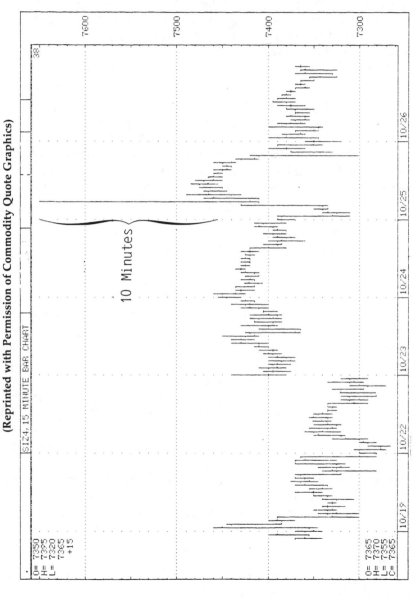

a period of 75 minutes! Then prices dropped from the 765 high to a daily low of 730 in 3½ hours, only to again run up 106 ($500 per contract) in 30 minutes. An examination of the price every five minutes (Figure 10–2) shows that the large move actually happened over a period of 10 minutes.

Though these moves have been intentionally selected to make a point, they are not uncommon. The futures trader who hesitates has lost a vital opportunity to make a high percentage on invested money. In this case, for example, assume it took the trader five minutes to decide that he should follow his signal to buy silver. Assume it took him another two minutes to have his buy order executed. It is now eight minutes into a 10-minute move. Had the trader been buying at the market, he would have bought at or close to the top, eventually ending up with a loss rather than a profit.

WHY TRADERS FAIL

As you can plainly see, the qualities required for success in futures trading are just as important as, if not more important than, the system one decides to use. The analogy I like to use in discussing the trader and the system is that of the car and the driver. In order to win a race, you may spend millions on perfecting the ultimate vehicle. Yet, if you have a poor driver, or one who cannot effectively manipulate the powerful vehicle through competition, traffic, danger and adverse weather, you will not win the race and your investment in the ultimate vehicle will be a waste! This is why so many people fail in the futures market or, for that matter, in every form of investment.

Taking the car and driver analogy one step further, you can see that a good driver, in an average vehicle, can actually win the race. Car and driver are inseparable, just as system and trader are. There is a strong, subtle, and pervasive interaction of the two, where one influences the other. You cannot have one without the other. I maintain, therefore, that in the investment and speculation worlds, too much attention has been given to the car and very little attention to the driver.

The world is full of investors and traders who, were it not for their blindness to their own shortcomings and subsequent trading habits, could be very successful. I have found that the system is not

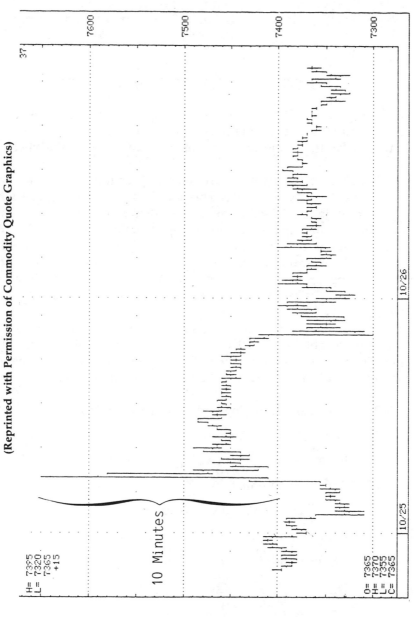

FIGURE 10–2 FIVE-MINUTE CHART SHOWING CLOSE UP OF
SILVER PRICE MOVEMENT IN GIGURE 9–1
(Reprinted with Permission of Commodity Quote Graphics)

nearly as important as the trader. In answer to the question, "Why do so many people fail?" I say simply that they have not learned the necessary skills to become winners. Winners are created, not born.

HOW TO IDENTIFY INCOMPETENCE

At the risk of offending my audience, I will say that you most likely know where you are lacking in confidence. If you don't, take a bit of time to examine some of the traits I've outlined in the checklist below.

Let's face it, the greatest part of starting on the road to success is getting off the road to failure. This requires you to recognize what road you're on. You need to make sure that your map fits the territory. The car-and-driver analogy is applicable here as well. If you're driving from point A to point B and you get lost, you may eventually find your way through luck. This, however, is unlikely. The only effective and prompt way to find the proper direction (before you run out of gas) is by asking someone who knows and then following the directions.

It is also true in futures trading. A "reality check" is essential. You must be able to honestly assess your character limitations. The checklist, if answered honestly, will help you admit to problems you may now have. In recognizing them, half the battle will be won.

1. I have trouble getting and staying organized.

2. I have difficulty planning the future.

3. I have been accused of acting on impulse.

4. I have limited time to work on the markets.

5. I am impatient with myself and others.

6. I tend to think too much and over-analyze.

7. I've been told that I give up too easily.

8. I feel insecure when I disagree with the majority.

9. I feel good when my broker agrees with my trading decisions.

10. It is more important to be lucky than good.

11. Most of my business ventures have met with failure.

12. I need a top trading system to win in the futures markets.

13. I tend to get frustrated quickly.

14. Many times I get overwhelmed and cannot act.

15. I do not like making decisions.

16. I tend to make poor decisions under pressure.

17. I feel depressed and resigned when I am wrong.

18. My self-esteem is dependent on what others think of me.

19. I tend to procrastinate.

20. I look to blame others for my mistakes.

21. I feel sorry for myself when things are not working out.

22. I oftentimes experience extreme emotional swings.

23. I have trouble with commitments.

24. I do not respect other people.

25. I idolize other people and their ideas.

26. I have too much pride and cannot readily admit when I am wrong.

27. I manage money poorly. I am overly wasteful or miserly.

28. I am not good at making or keeping promises.

29. I do not manage stress well.

30. I tend to be prejudiced and stubborn in my views.

31. I do not like learning new things.

32. I cannot afford to lose too much money in futures trading.

Though by no means exhaustive, the listing in Figure 10–3 will act as a very quick screening test for success. I have found that if 27 or more of your answers to the questions above are "yes," then you have much to work on before you can begin trading. The best thing this book can do for you, above and beyond the simple mechanics of trading, is to let you know whether or not you are ready to begin trading.

Regardless of how ready you think you will be, the acid test of trading with your own money always creates pressures that you have not previously experienced. Preparation, planning, personality change, and perseverance are the 4 Ps of trading that must be learned by all who seek success in futures or, for that matter, in any business venture.

Now that you've been honest with yourself, and confessed to some of your shortcomings in life and in the marketplace, we can begin some preliminary work on how to improve and trade like a professional. Let me say, for starters, that I am assuming you have a system that is correct at least 60 percent of the time. Here is a starting list of practices you can now begin in order to improve on your eventual trading success.

1. **Develop an Organized Style.**
    Organization is vital to the success of any venture. It is important to know where you are headed, when you expect to get there, and which vehicles you will use to reach your destination. Without organization, these tools can often be misplaced. Your charts, books, formulae, trading rules, and telephone numbers must be readily available and organized. There are many details to think about while trading. Creating an organized environment can free your concentration for the important things.

2. **Develop and Practice Discipline.**
    There are many ways to develop your discipline. One of them is to take a course on self-improvement, such as those offered by the Dale Carnegie Institute. You will learn that

success requires discipline and that discipline can be learned. Discipline can often be improved through the simple application of behavioral learning techniques. My book, *The Investor's Quotient* (New York: John Wiley & Sons, 1980), gives specific suggestions and techniques designed to help you improve your discipline. In addition, there are many simple exercises that you can use.

Remember that discipline from one area of your life tends to be reflected in all others. Therefore, if you lack self-discipline when it comes to changing such negative habits as excessive drinking, overeating, and smoking, then you will probably lack the discipline required for successful trading. You may need to overcome these habits first, or you may need to conquer all lack of discipline at once.

Finally, remember that discipline is not synonymous with rigidity. Being rigid in following rules is not necessarily a form of discipline. Being a disciplined trader also means being flexible enough to change course as soon as you see that the action you have taken is not working. The rigid trader will believe too strongly in his or her trading rules and this can prove destructive. Trading is a game of probability and there is no room for rigidity when it comes to probability.

3. **Develop a Simple and Effective Trading Approach.**
   One of the greatest limitations on success in trading is that systems become too complicated, too burdensome, or too time-consuming to use. If you build a boat, make certain you can get your boat into the water. Once in the water, make certain you can move.

   Too many traders spend too much time developing complicated, sophisticated trading systems that are too difficult to implement. My knowledge of top-ranking, successful futures traders shows that most of them use simple methods. You will hear "keep it simple" repeated again and again.

This should be remembered and applied when developing your trading approach. If you keep it simple you will be less consumed with details, less troubled with self-discipline, and you will shorten your market response time. This alone will prove very valuable.

4. **Learn to Isolate and Monitor Impulsive Behavior.**
    There's a great deal to be said for isolationism in trading. In order to keep free of impulse, it is often best to not know the news. Then you can "keep your head while all those around you are losing theirs." You will, in so doing, avoid the costly errors that are so often the result of impulsive behavior rather than following your system.

    I favor isolation. I prefer not to listen to the radio or television news. I do not read the newspapers, or listen to the opinions of others. In particular, I do not discuss the markets, even with other professionals. I isolate because I know that I may be influenced by the information. In order to be strong and avoid impulsive actions motivated by the emotions of fear and/or greed, I must limit my exposure to extraneous information.

5. **Plan Your Trades and Trade Your Plans.**
    This market cliche is just as true today as when it was coined. It is the best way to avoid virtually all of the losing inputs. If you are prepared, and if you act according to your plan, you will have taken the first and most important step to practicing self-discipline.

6. **Keep Your Objectives Clearly in Mind.**
    Chapter 17 discusses trading objectives. You must first define your goals and then keep them always in mind. If you are a short-term trader, then you must think and act like one. This means maintaining a consistent, short-term time horizon in all your trading. However, if you're a long-term trader, then your perception of the markets and your corresponding actions must be consistent with long-term time ho-

rizons. Have your main objectives set, your goals organized in a way that supports your objectives, and make sure you develop a system that checks for consistency. It is easy to get sidetracked from your goals. Maintaining consistency by asking yourself if the day-to-day actions support your goals will help keep you on track. I have found it best to have a list of objectives and goals handy for quick reference during times of need.

7. **Manage Your Stress, and Do Not Take the Markets Home with You.**
In order to improve market decisions, it is necessary to deal effectively with stress. There are many ways in which this can be done. Exercise is one good way to cope with stress. It can help you vent frustrations and give you a chance to get your mind off the markets. It is also helpful to manage your psychological stress when you experience losses. Undoubtedly, you will experience a number of losses and it is necessary to learn not to take these losses personally. If you do not learn this, stress will build and your confidence will falter.

Leave the markets at the office. If you plan to trade as your profession, then this rule is vital. If you plan to trade in your spare time, then have certain hours set aside for this activity and do not become addicted to the market.

8. **Keep Commission Costs Low.**
The overhead of trading consists of losses and commissions. Commissions comprise a built-in loss factor. Poor order execution comprises another aspect of the built-in cost of doing business. Between poor order fills and commissions, about 25 percent of profits can be eaten up before your very eyes.

Many traders are shocked when they see how much they've paid out in commissions every year. Some traders who want and need the advice of brokers will need to do business with a "full service house." They will, therefore, pay higher commissions. There's nothing wrong with this provided it is cost-effective. If you deal with a full-service house and pay higher commissions, it doesn't necessarily mean you will fail. However, you must get some return for what you are paying in higher costs. If you do not get a return, then you're not making a sound business decision. If you trade frequently without needing advice or information, then you are entitled to lower commissions. You can ask your full-service broker for a discount. Be informed about their discount policies. Don't be afraid to ask how much trading you will need to do in order to benefit from the commission break.

Finally, if you see that you are not using any of the information put out by the house you're dealing with, take the time to investigate another house offering discount commissions. But first, inquire with your current broker to determine if he can lower his rates, since a good broker/trader relationship is very important. Chapter 12 covers these issues in detail.

9. **Avoid Over-Trading—Be Conservative.**
   One of the greatest secrets to success in trading is to avoid "over-trading." This mistake is caused by the erroneous assumption that you must be in every market at all times. There is no substance or truth to this belief. As a matter of fact, market professionals like to concentrate on certain markets and only on certain types of moves.

   Another pitfall for many traders is they over-trade in order to feel involved. They become addicted to the excitement of big positions and constant action. They live by the motto, "If you're not afraid, you are not paying attention." The market is a dangerous place to play this type of game.

   You cannot and should not be in all markets at all times. And you are risking too much when you over-trade in terms of volume. Therefore, be conservative and trade manageably, with only the best signals and the most reasonable risk-to-reward ratios. This is discussed in various chapters throughout the book.

10. Avoid Wishful Thinking.

Most unsuccessful traders get stuck in trades that are going against them and begin to hope things will change. They lose all concept of discipline, rigor, and rules. Wishful thinking is, in essence, rationalization, a distorted view of reality and, most often, will lead to failure. Anytime traders allow their thinking to be guided by hope, they are resorting to fantasy, rather than reality.

Markets have their own logic, fleeting as it may be at times. Chances are, the market is not listening or responding to your internal messages of hope. You are better off checking in with reality, your equity. Determine to shift your thinking away from hopes and wishes and back toward the market.

SUMMARY

In order to be successful in the futures markets, there are many modes of behaviors you will need to cultivate and others you will need to eliminate. Identifying your strengths and weaknesses and learning the steps toward developing a winning attitude were discussed. This chapter provided a checklist designed to help you evaluate yourself, and it made suggestions for changing some of the behaviors and attitudes you may now have that can prevent successful trading and speculation in futures and options.

Chapter

11

Tools for Successful Trading

The student of futures trading has a very clear and concise goal. This goal is not primarily to beat the market or to become skillful for the sake of skill alone. The true speculator is, first and foremost, interested in profits and success.

As you can tell from your own trading experience, from other aspects of life, and from my many caveats in this book, there is no surefire or simple road to success in the markets. With so many techniques to choose from, with so many different orientations, and with so many trading systems available to speculators, what you ultimately develop will be an individual, tailor-made approach designed specifically to suit your purposes. Whether you end up with a purely mechanical approach based on the research of others, or a primarily subjective approach based on your own interpretations and studies, the fact remains that the ultimate decision-making is yours and yours alone.

Yet, regardless of what you select or how you select it, you can readily see from what you have already read in this book, and from what you may already know, that there are some common threads that weave through every approach to futures trading. These commonalties influence and regulate the success or failure of virtually every trader.

While it may be true that some individuals achieve success by breaking all the rules, it is also true that such individuals are clearly in the minority, and that their success is the exception, rather than the rule. Unless you are blessed with fantastic luck, you will need to achieve success in the futures markets the good old-fashioned way: you will have to earn it. The only way to earn lasting success is through the diligent and disciplined application of specific techniques and methods, few of which are directly related to systems, and most of which are clearly the function of attitudes, psychology, and discipline.

You may not want to hear this, but the fact is that it matters little what system or systems you select, how tremendous their hypothetical performance may be, or how well others may have done with these systems. What ultimately matters is how you apply the systems, and the consistency with which you can put the techniques into operation.

The human being is not a computer, and he or she cannot achieve the same level of perfection that may be required to institute a trading system in complete accordance with the ideal conditions under which it was tested. The degree of slippage, drawdown, and trader error are often significant. Furthermore, it frequently seems that real-time market conditions deteriorate the performance of most systems. In fact, no system based on hypothetical or computer-simulated or tested results can be taken as worthwhile unless these results can be replicated with reasonable similarity in real time.

It is for these reasons that the steps toward trading success do not rest exclusively, or for that matter heavily, upon selection of a trading system. Though I know that the selection of a system is important, I suspect that its value has been overstated, particularly by those with a vested interest in selling systems, or in managing a fund based on such systems. In order to achieve success it will be necessary for you to follow most, if not all, of the time-tested rules of profitable trading.

Though I will begin my list with items related to system selection, you will observe that these items do not dominate the list. Remember also that variations on each item in the list are certainly possible in order to adapt them to your particular situation.

TOOLS FOR BETTER TRADING

1. Find or develop a trading system that has a real-time record (or computer-tested record) of 60 percent or more winning trades, with a ratio of approximately 2 to 1 in terms of dollars made versus dollars lost per trade (including commissions and slippage as losses). In the absence of real-time results, computer results are acceptable, provided you have made provisions for their limitations as discussed earlier in this book. Though the figures just given need not be replicated exactly, attempt to get close.

2. The system you find or develop should be consistent with your time limitations or availability (with or without a computer system). If the signals are generated by an advisory service, then make certain you have familiarized yourself with the basics of the system, its trading approach, and other details of the system as described earlier in the text.

3. Select a brokerage firm that will be compatible with your needs. If you are an independent trader and need no input whatsoever, then select a discount firm that gives good service and prompt order executions. If, however, you are a novice trader requiring a full-service firm, then be willing to pay higher commissions in order to have your needs fulfilled.

4. Select a specific broker within the firm, or specify your needs to the firm if you will not be working with one particular broker. Make certain that both you and the broker are aware of each other's needs, and keep the lines of communication clear.

5. Make certain you have sufficient risk capital to trade the system you have selected. Be certain that your risk capital is

truly risk capital and not funds upon which you are otherwise counting on for some future purpose.

6. Develop and formulate your trading philosophy. As you know, your perceptions of trading, your expectations, your goals, and your market orientation (i.e., long-term, short-term) are all factors that contribute either to success or to failure.

7. Plan your trades and follow through on your plans. Attempt not to trade on whim. Rather, work from a trading plan every day so you will avoid the temptation of making spur-of-the-moment decisions that are not based on any system or method you are using.

8. Be an isolationist. There is great value in being a loner when it comes to speculation. You don't necessarily want anyone else's input. You don't necessarily want anyone else's opinions. As time goes on, as the lessons you learn begin to accumulate, you will realize that your own good opinion is just as valuable, perhaps more so, than the opinions of any others—experts or novices.

9. Make a commitment; take the plunge! Make a commitment to trading. The commitment should consist of rules, organizational procedures, goals, and expectations. Delineate these carefully, with consideration and with forethought. By making your plans, you will avoid costly errors that are not consistent with your plans.

10. Once you've decided—act! Don't hesitate a moment once your trading decision has been made (whether the decision is to get into a trade or to get out of a trade). It matters not whether you are taking a profit or closing out a loss. As soon as you have a clear-cut signal to act, don't hesitate. Act as soon as your system says you must act—no sooner, no later.

11. Limit risk and preserve capital. The best way to limit risk is to trade only in three to six markets at once and to avoid trading markets that have swings much too large for your account size. Once you have decided to limit risk to a certain dollar amount, or to limit risk using a specific technique, make certain you take your losses as soon as they should be taken. Do this on time—not too soon, not too late!

12. Don't anticipate. Many traders go astray when they anticipate signals from their trading system. The trading system is your traffic light. The traffic is always heavy. Stop on the red, go on the green, be cautious on yellow. If you anticipate trading signals from your system, you might as well not have a system at all.

13. The market is the master, you are the slave. Like it or not, you cannot tell the market what to do. It will always do what it wants and it is your job to figure out what it is doing. Once done, you must follow the market through its many twists and turns. If it is zigging and zagging, then you must zig and zag. If it is trending higher, you must trade from the long side. If it is trending lower, you must trade from the short side.

    It may be instructive for you to review, from time to time, which side of the market most of your trades were on. If you find that you have been bucking the trend of the market, then you must review either your system or your discipline. One of the two (perhaps both) are not functioning properly. Many traders have gone astray by failing to follow the market, thinking that it is their job to forecast the market. The job of the trader is to follow, not to forecast. Let's leave forecasting to the economists.

14. Do your homework. Whether you are using a computer or pen and pencil, whether you are a novice or a seasoned veteran, you must keep your research current. Futures mar-

kets move so fast that there is precious little time to update your trading signals once a move has occurred. You must be there at the very inception of a move or shortly thereafter. Otherwise you will have difficulty getting aboard for the bigger move. The only way to do this is to keep your home-work up to date. If you have a computer it may be easier. You can program your computer so it will automatically update your signals or system every day at a certain time. Regardless, discipline is always involved and you must keep current.

15. Avoid extremes in emotion. The greatest friend of the specu-lator is the emotion of others; emotion within the speculator is one of his or her greatest enemies. When trading, emo-tions must be under control and they must be ignored. Re-gardless of the trend of emotions, their consequences can be exceptionally dangerous to the speculator since they can re-sult in unwarranted actions. I have commented on this throughout the book.

16. Assume responsibility for all your of trading activity. Ac-cepting that you alone are responsible for the outcome of your trading is a major step toward achieving success. Many traders are unaware that they put a psychological barrier between the actions they take and the results of these ac-tions. They look to blame other people, the market, or any-thing else that will remove the focus of responsibility from themselves. Becoming rigorously honest and "owning" your actions will lead to consistency and success in the markets.

17. Hope and fear limit your attention to the market. Both attitudes turn a trader into a passive player. When you hope a position will go your way, or fear that it will go against you, you abandon your ability to think and take action. Hope and fear are similar and will produce behavior that is paralyzing for the trader. Inability to respond to changing market conditions will destroy a trader's confidence and lead to substantial losses.

18. Avoid overconfidence—it will breed complacency. I have often heard of traders who have a string of good trades, which invariably is followed by a big loss. Why does this happen? The emotional "high" of achieving success in the market can lead to such a feeling of satisfaction that one actually becomes lazy. The market is oblivious to your experience of success or failure and therefore demands that you always pay attention when you are involved. Allowing your judgment to be impaired by any emotional extreme will precipitate hazardous trading.

19. Monitor your performance and pay attention to results. The rate and frequency of change that takes place within futures markets is unlike most other environments. The opportunity for a trader to receive constant and instantaneous feedback is always present. How much and how often a trader wants to observe this fact and learn from his or her actions is another question. It has been said that trading the markets is similar to getting a report card every day. The ability to take advantage of this feedback and learn from it will lead to increased confidence and success in the markets.

20. Develop positive relationships. People influence how we look at the world and how we think about ourselves. Friends often act as a mirror of our own reality. Consequently, it is important to surround ourselves with people who have a healthy and positive sense of themselves. If we associate with people who complain, blame, gossip, or just plain "quit," we will be influenced by their behavior. Moods are contagious and if we surround ourselves with negative people, we will eventually become negative. As traders, therefore, it is critical to be aware of the company we keep and to be with those who maintain a healthy and winning attitude.

21. Don't trade on tips, "sure things," or inside information. The temptation in all of us is to find the easy way. But you know the easy way is rarely the best way. There will always be

lottery winners, but your odds of winning any lottery are slim. Therefore, avoid the temptation of taking tips, following inside information, listening to the opinions of other traders, or believing that the person you are listening to or talking to knows more than you do. Sometimes they do, but most of the time they don't. Collective opinions are, of course, helpful in the case of contrary opinion studies, but individual opinions or tips are basically useless to the trader.

22. When you make money, take some of it away from the market. When you have been doing well, remember to systematically remove money from your account. Whether you do this on a profitable trade basis or on a time basis (i.e., daily, weekly, monthly) is not important. What is important is to do it.

Traders have winning and losing periods. During the winning times, profits will accumulate rapidly and before you know it you may become impressed with your success. You will examine ways to expand your trading in view of your tremendous profits. You will look at how much money there is in your account and you will be tempted to trade larger positions.

While there will be a time for this, it is usually not right to do so when you are feeling exceptionally euphoric about your performance. One way to reduce euphoria and put profits away for a rainy day is by having a systematic method of withdrawing profits.

23. Develop winning attitudes and behaviors. You can do this by reading the writings of the great traders. Spend more time developing yourself than you do developing your systems. The key variable in the trading success equation is the trader and not the system. I maintain that a good trader can make virtually any system work.

24. "The trend is your friend." This old expression is known to all, but used by few. Whether you allow the major trend to filter signals from your system as the final deciding factor, or whether you use a system that is based entirely on trend-following principles, always be cautious when your trades are not consistent with the existing trend. Naturally, there will be times when your signals are against the trend. There will be times when the trend is apt to change. However, you should always be careful about trades and signals against the trend since they will most often be wrong.

25. Don't try to trade too many markets. There are many different markets, but most move together. There are only a few major market groups. Take one market from each group, preferably the most active, and focus on it. Few traders can be involved in all markets at once.

26. Don't take the market home with you. Futures trading can be a consuming business and whether you are trading well or not, it is advisable to get into the habit of leaving the markets at the office. Do not carry the effects of your trading into other aspects of your life. If you are trading well you may become complacent in areas where you need to work. Conversely, trading poorly can often lead you to feel depressed and not motivated to take care of other concerns in your life. Try to keep work separate from other areas, and reserve time to take vacations and get away from the trading environment.

27. Don't lose sight of your goals. Your goal in futures trading is to make money. There is no goal greater than this in futures trading. Though there may be other benefits such as self-satisfaction, the thrill of trading, and the sublimation of hostility and competitive instincts, these are all secondary. If you seek revenge against the market or other traders, if you wish merely to compete for the sake of competition, or to trade only for the thrill of trading, then the primary goal of speculation will be lost and so will your money!

SUMMARY

The rules presented in this chapter are based on my many experiences and observations in futures trading since 1968. Though some rules may be more important to you than others, I know that at one time or another, all of these will be important to all traders. The best way to employ these rules in your trading program is to study them, to keep them at your disposal and to review them regularly. They will help keep you on the right track and they will help keep you honest with yourself.

Perhaps one of the greatest errors a speculator can commit is self-deception. The markets are brutal and the pain of losses is omnipresent. No trader or speculator is immune to losses. What ultimately separates the winners from the losers is the ability to be honest with oneself. From this rare quality arises clear perception. From a clear perception of reality emanates the ability to use only what is effective and to discard all that is not.

Part

3

The Mechanics of Trading

Chapter

12

What You Need to Know about Market Information Services and Brokers

There are many decisions to make when you first begin trading. One important consideration is to select the right information service. This is an important decision to make as it can not only save you considerable time and effort, it can also help you to make money. Another decision you need to make is choosing the proper broker suitable for your style of trading. This chapter seeks to inform you of the types of services available and the things you need to be aware of in selecting a broker.

WHY USE A SERVICE?

The first consideration in purchasing any type of service connected with futures trading is its ability to help save you time. If you can purchase a service for several hundred dollars a year, then you are practicing good business sense. A good information service will save you time and energy in learning about the markets. Today there are many active markets, with many different contract months, futures options, etc. The individual speculator can purchase considerable market information on a regular basis at a reasonable cost, thereby avoiding the time, expense, and effort involved in producing the information manually or with one's own computer system.

It should be remembered that many times the speculator may wish to do his or her own homework, since this is frequently a very good way to keep in touch with the markets. In particular, individuals whose main method of trading is charting should spend at least their early months of trading doing their own charts, since much will be learned from observing how the basic chart patterns develop. These basic understandings and skills will build the foundation to understand higher level concepts down the road. This is why I strongly recommend that each speculator spend some time manually calculating (if possible) some of his or her indicators. I myself have had many insights about the market while manually computing indicators and signals. For the chartist, the benefits of a service may be enhanced after an initial period of manual updates.

WHAT YOU NEED TO KNOW ABOUT INFORMATION SERVICES

Without citing specific services by name, I will attempt to acquaint you with the following aspects of the services available by including:

1. The types of services available.

2. Different features of the various services.

3. What to look for in a service.

4. Ideas that may help you save time and money.

TYPES OF SERVICES

I categorize futures services into two basic groups, (a) those that provide strictly factual information (i.e., charts and statistics), and (b) those that provide interpretive market information. It is interesting to note that many services that do not consider themselves interpretive in nature are, in fact, just that. Of further interest is the fact that the Commodity Futures Trading Commission and the National Futures Association, both futures regulatory agencies, require advisory services to be registered in order to disseminate their information. However, many services that are, in fact, advisory in nature are not required to register as advisors.

INFORMATION SERVICES

There are essentially three types of informational services. They are:

1. Purely statistical services (fundamental and technical).

2. Chart services.

3. News services.

1. **Statistical Services**
   Essentially, statistical services do nothing but report statistics. The statistics may be technical or fundamental, but the key element here is that they do not offer any interpretation of the statistics; they merely report them as they have occurred. In this category, I would include both fundamentally and technically oriented statistical services.

   Statistical services may include such things as government reports, government statistics, Commitment of Traders Reports, shipping information, crop reports, and planting intentions. Any report that provides merely factual information is considered informational and not interpretative. One should be aware that many services that provide such data also offer their own interpretation of the data. This kind of service I consider to be somewhat advisory in nature, depending upon the fashion in which the information has been reported.

2. **Chart Services**
   The area of chart services covers a wide variety of publications. There is, however, a very clear distinction between chart services that merely report factual information, and chart services that interpret and advise based on the chart information. The distinction is important, since the independent futures trader does not wish to clutter his or her mind with opinions or analyses prepared by others. This is very important (as you will recall) to the truly independent trader.

It is interesting to note that some services that in the past were purely informational have slowly become more advisory oriented. However, they still separate their chart analyses physically from their charts. This is helpful to the independent trader who can simply separate the recommendations and opinions from the charts and dispose of the recommendations in order to avoid being influenced by them.

Ideally, however, I would recommend that the trader who wishes to make his or her decisions totally uninfluenced by the input of other analysts subscribe to a chart service that is purely informational, containing no chart analyses whatsoever.

An interesting sidelight of chart services has developed in recent years. It is becoming more fashionable for them to also include various market indicators in chart form along with the charts. These indicators may be helpful to some traders. However, as is the case of market opinions, I find that they are best avoided by the truly independent speculator. As you can well imagine, indicators of such a nature can influence you in both subtle and overt ways.

Please understand that I am not deeming these indicators useless, nor do I advise all traders to avoid them. I am, however, alerting you to the fact that many traders may not wish to have such input unless they feel they need the additional information, or they are interested in supplementing their market analyses with the input provided by indicators that they feel have good potential.

Other considerations in subscribing to a chart service are equally important. Perhaps the single greatest feature of any chart service is the user's ability to update his or her charts manually. The chart service should allow sufficient room to project cycles and trendlines into the future, as well as room on which to update the charts. The price scales should be easy to work with, and the paper should be thick enough to allow manual updates. Within reasonable limits, the larger the charts, the better. An important consideration that many traders have overlooked is the availability of opening prices on a daily price chart.

As I have demonstrated elsewhere in this book, opening prices are important to the speculator, perhaps more important than many analysts believe them to be. My preference is for a chart service containing them. Unfortunately, in today's chart service market, this narrows the available choices quite significantly, since most services do not plot opening prices. Certainly, their use is a matter of individual preference, but I suggest you give it strong consideration after reviewing some of my work and techniques using opening prices.

3. **News Services**
   In some respects, news services are similar to chart services. There are those that report the news and those that report *and* interpret the news. The caveats in this case are similar to those I outlined earlier for the two different types of chart

services. Again, an independent trader must evaluate the relevance of the information based on his or her specific needs. Many traders, in fact, prefer not to know the news since their approach is primarily technical.

ADVISORY SERVICES

The real issue is, do you want or do you need an advisory service? Remember that there are assets and liabilities regardless of which decision you may make. The benefits of having an advisory service are essentially threefold:

1. Many advisory services do full-time work on indicators and techniques that may be consistent with your orientation to the market. Consequently, you may save yourself considerable time by subscribing.

2. Many advisory services have good performance records that can help you profit in the markets. Just keep in mind, though, that all services have their good times as well as bad, just as traders do.

3. Advisory services may be valuable in helping your discipline. It is easier for some traders to follow the advice of another than it is for them to take their own good advice. All three points should be considered when making your decision.

    On the other hand, there are a number of points to consider on the negative side of advisory services.

1. **Dependency**
    Many traders do not look favorably upon the possibility of becoming dependent on an advisory service. Though the particular advisor or newsletter may be doing well at present, performance could change markedly over time. This is, of course, the risk one takes in depending upon someone else's advice.

2. **Lack of Teaching**

    The individual who subscribes to a service that does nothing more than make recommendations, providing minimal analyses or justification for these recommendations, may find him- or herself not learning anything from the service. Individuals who are in the futures markets in order to further their understanding, and who plan at some point to develop an independent approach, will not benefit from such services.

3. **Results**

    It can often be difficult to duplicate the results of some advisory services. This could be due to a number of factors including trader discipline or inaccurate/misrepresented reporting of results. Before considering an advisory service, verify performance claims through an independent evaluating service (if one is available for the service you are considering). Be certain that slippage and commissions are counted as part of the losses.

4. **Methodological Considerations**

    In deciding to commit to a given advisory service or services, it is also important to carefully consider the systems or methods they plan to employ in their trading. In some cases, the methodology of the services is known and clearly stated for potential and current subscribers. In other instances, however, the service may wish to keep confidential most aspects of their approach, giving nothing but advice as to when to buy and/or sell. There is nothing wrong with either procedure.

    However, the secretive approach may not satisfy some individuals who feel they must know why they are committing their money. Furthermore, the secretive approach does not provide any educational benefits to the subscriber. You may also want to know the overall risk management philosophy and therefore you would want to know the specifics of the trading.

EVALUATING A SERVICE

With so many services available to today's futures trader, I would recommend you follow a number of specific steps and procedures before selecting a service. Understand that, although I have a vested interest since I publish several advisory services for speculators, I am attempting to give you a totally unbiased point of view since the topic is a very important one.

Before outlining a step-by-step procedure for you, you must remember that the basic question is, "Do you really want to subscribe to an advisory service?" The answer is strictly an individual one that must take into consideration your own needs, assets, strengths, and weaknesses. Please remember that my purpose is to provide you with a truthful answer, and not one that will serve my purposes. I am certain that I speak for a majority of trading advisors who publish newsletters when I say that we do not want to entice subscribers to our service unless they can truly employ it either as part of their own research or trade exclusively with our recommendations.

The ultimate goal is for everyone to profit; subscribers and newsletter writers alike. None of us want unhappy subscribers who do not feel that what they have purchased is to their benefit. This is why I would rather discourage someone at the start, as opposed to enticing individuals who are really not ready for an advisory service.

Given the fact that many individuals want to trade futures, but are limited in the time they can devote to a futures analysis, the need arises for an advisory-type service. Individuals who cannot make the time commitment are, therefore, drawn to services that are akin to their market orientations. Those who follow cycles, for example, may be attracted to one type of service, whereas individuals who are more interested in fundamentals may be attracted to a different type. There is a market advisory service available for virtually every type of market orientation covering everything from fundamentals to astrological systems. With this background in mind, and with the full realization that advisory services are not for all speculators, here are a number of points to consider in selecting a service.

1. **Specificity**
   Some advisory services claim fantastic performance records

that, upon closer examination, are discovered to be based on very general recommendations, and leave too much of the decision-making process to the reader. Vague recommendations can be interpreted in many different ways and the individual making these recommendations can make virtually any claim with 20/20 hindsight. Therefore, when considering a service, make certain that its recommendations are specific regarding entry, exit, and follow-up. Such specificity can be in the form of specific price orders, or in specific market instructions (i.e., buy on Monday's open).

2. **Timeliness**
   Some advisory services are not sufficiently timely to permit real-time implementation. Either their timely advice is received by subscribers too late, or their recommendations are made too late to permit real-time implementation. Ideally, you should either be able to maintain close touch with your advisory service on a daily basis or the recommendations provided in their newsletter should be so specific and with such close follow-up that telephone contact would be unnecessary.

3. **Objectives, Stops, Alternatives**
   A good advisory service should provide you with all three of these. Ideally you should have price or time objectives, stops, and specific follow-up procedures that will leave you with alternatives regardless of market conditions. If you are going to pay an advisor, then make sure you are paying for a complete package. Some services are wonderful at getting you into the market, but vague and nonspecific when it comes to getting you out.

4. **Cost**
   The cost of some services may be prohibitive in terms of what you get. While it is true that each service is unique in the information it provides, the cost of what you get may not turn out to be effective in terms of how you use the information, or of the extent to which the information proves

profitable. Unfortunately, it is impossible to know this in advance. Rather, you will need to make this evaluation at regular intervals once you have found a service that suits your needs.

5. **Portfolio Size**
   Some advisory services with excellent performance records have achieved their hypothetical results in a fashion that cannot be duplicated by most speculators. In some cases, they have taken on extremely large positions, scaled into the market holding losing positions, hypothetically purchased or sold extremely large numbers of contracts, or added more and more margin to their hypothetical account until they have weathered most storms. Since this is not a realistic way for the average trader to approach the market, it is not sug- gested that you follow the work of a service such as this. I'm aware of several services that have practiced such proce- dures in one form or another (sometimes in all forms). With- out naming names, I recommend you be aware.

   Realistically, most futures portfolios should not contain more than five to ten positions at any time. That's just my orientation, but I think you'll find this approach makes sense for most speculators.

6. **Hotline**
   Does the service have a hotline you can call at least daily in order to obtain the latest recommendations, updates, and follow-ups? The recorder is a good way to keep in touch with your service and its recommendations. However, a hotline is not necessary if the service can maintain a thor- ough follow-up in its newsletter. Note that some recorder hotlines are essentially useless since they do not provide specific recommendations. Rather, they provide nothing but general comments.

7. **Performance Record**
   You will observe that performance record is not one of the

major items on my list, yet it is important. Provided the performance record is honestly reported and truly representative of the service's record, you should consider its history carefully. The would-be subscriber who looks merely at the bottom line may be in for a rude awakening when he or she actually subscribes to the service.

You must examine in close detail such items as the largest single loss, the largest single profit, the average loss, the average profit and the win/lose percentage ratio. The reasons for doing so should be abundantly clear to you if you have been reading previous chapters in this book carefully. It is important to remember that a service that makes most of its profits on a few highly profitable trades may not be the best service for you. The rule of thumb in assessing the potential of any service in your program is whether you can duplicate its results. If you can, then the service is for you. If, however, the results would be difficult for you to replicate, then you are best advised to look elsewhere.

8. **Deduction for Commissions**
Read the fine print! Some services do not deduct exceptionally large commissions from their performance records. Other services do not deduct any commissions from their performance records.

9. **Price Fills**
In assessing realistic representation of recommendations, be sure to look for hypothetical price fills. Some services claim recommendations being filled on entry and/or exit when, in fact, such fills may not have been possible at the stated price. Consider this in evaluating your subscription to a service.

10. **Which Markets Are Traded?**
Some services specialize in only certain markets. It may be that the markets that are the specialty of a certain service are either too risky or too volatile for you. You can determine this fact from examining the performance record and from

studying the service's promotional literature. Also bear in mind that the service may make recommendations in particularly thin markets, which may also not be to your liking. Advisory service recommendations to a large audience in a thin market can certainly result in exceptionally bad price executions on entry and exit. Do not subscribe to a service that is not consistent with your needs, general expectations, and orientation regarding specific markets covered.

While this list is not exhaustive, these are some of the items different services offer. While a good information service can be a help, traders should realize that, ultimately, they need to trust their own judgment. Whether you subscribe to a good service, have a good system, or have a good broker, nothing will help if you cannot trust your own decisions.

FINDING A BROKER

From my observation, one of the most misunderstood things about futures trading, aside from the placement of orders, is the relationship between broker and client. In order to fully understand this relationship, it is important to understand the differences among types of customers. The relationship between broker and client can prove to be your greatest asset or greatest liability. This is why I strongly suggest that you do not take the issue of selecting a broker lightly. Many decisions must be made, and they must be made correctly as early in the game as possible.

WHAT TYPE OF TRADER ARE YOU?

The first decision you must make is the kind of trader you are and would like to be, and where you plan to go with your trading. There are several types of traders. The following is a list of their characteristics:

1. **The Novice**
   This trader has little or no experience, feels nervous, uncertain and insecure, and is likely lacking in knowledge. This type of individual needs a broker who "holds his or her hand," who is patient and familiar with the concerns of the novice trader.

2. **Experienced Short-Term Trader**
   This individual has considerable experience and is primarily interested in quick trading (usually intraday or over a period of several days). Such an individual would require no input from a broker and may only require quotes and good execution.

3. **The Long-Term Trader**
   This individual does not trade often and may require specialized services from a broker such as statistical and/or fundamental information.

4. **The Independent Trader**
   Regardless of market orientation, many traders prefer to be totally independent and seek no input from their broker. Such individuals should select a broker for order-taking purposes only.

Essentially, these are the four types of traders common in today's markets. There are those who seek to have broker input and those who are not interested in any information from their broker. The broker who provides information, quotes, ideas, etc., should be reimbursed for additional services, whereas the broker who provides nothing but price fills should be able to provide lower commissions. Hence, the distinction between "full-service brokers" and "discount brokers."

Full-Service Brokers

Full-service brokerage firms pride themselves on producing research, providing quotes to clients through their brokers, and frequently maintaining one or several managed account programs.

Discount Brokers

Discount brokers, both in stocks and futures, charge significantly lower commission rates than do full-service firms. While most discount firms do not provide research, some have recently moved to a sliding scale under which they provide additional services such as research and broker input. Similarly, many full service firms are now discounting their commissions to customers who do not require additional services.

The commission price war has gone about as far as it can go, but it still is in the trader's best interest to explore and ask questions concerning the type of broker he or she needs. In addition to the factors mentioned, pay particular attention to (a) the financial stability of the firm, (b) commission structure, and (c) the different services you need.

DISCRETIONARY ACCOUNTS

The discretionary or managed account takes all decision-making functions and controls away from the customer, and puts them into the hands of a pro. This may be a group or individual who will exercise control over the account. The trades are managed by this group or individual and, with the exception of when to add or take money from the account, the decisions are controlled by them.

BROKER/CLIENT RELATIONSHIPS

Before closing this chapter, I would like to give you just a few thoughts about the broker/client relationship. The many different types of customers and brokers and their different interactions allow for many different types of broker/client relationships. The most important element to establish is trust. Without trust, you may sabotage your own trading. It is necessary, therefore, to be clear and up-front about your needs and expectations. The clearer you can be about your style of trading, the services you require, and the commission you are willing to pay, the better chance you have of developing a good relationship with your broker.

SUMMARY

This chapter reviewed the different types of services available to the commodity trader. Readers were advised as to selection of the appropriate service for their type of trading. It was also explored whether a service is even necessary. The importance of selecting a broker was highlighted along with distinctions between the full-service broker and the discount broker. The importance of self-trust and self-confidence were stressed in the search for finding an information services broker.

Chapter

13

What You Need to Know about Placing Orders

One of the most critically important but least understood aspects of futures trading is the use of price orders. Oftentimes traders misunderstand the meaning of certain orders and, upon receiving a bad order fill, tend to blame their broker. In fact, a thorough knowledge of order placement can prevent much aggravation, as well as many poor price fills.

In order to understand orders better, let's follow an order from its inception to its culmination. Let's assume you call your broker and place an order to buy one contract of March Treasury bond futures "at the market." Specifically, this means you will buy at whatever price can be obtained for you when your order reaches the floor of the exchange or the trading pit (the difference to be explained later).

The order-entry process begins with your call to your broker. You pick up the phone and call your broker. "Buy one March T Bond at the market," is the instruction. Depending on the type of trading you do and the type of broker you have, you will either hang up the phone or you will hold on for your price fill.

When your broker receives the order, he or she will write an order ticket containing your account number and your specific order. The ticket will then be time-stamped. Your broker will call the order down to the floor of the exchange, where the ticket will be similarly written and handed to a runner.

The runner will take the ticket to the pit broker who will then execute your order, write the price fill on the ticket, and hand it back to the runner. The runner will take it back to the order desk on the floor. The floor desk will report back to your broker, who will then give you your price fill, either while you are waiting on the telephone or by calling you.

If you are doing business with a broker who can fill your order using arbitrage methods, the transactions just described will be somewhat different. Once your broker has the order and calls it down to the floor, an individual at the order desk on the floor will hand-signal the pit trader to execute your order. The pit trader will then execute it and, by hand signal, report the fill back to the order desk. In this way you can very frequently have your order filled and reported back to you most often in less than one minute. Arbitrage techniques are becoming more common in very active markets such as Standard & Poor's futures and Treasury bond futures.

Other types of orders such as those above the market, below the market, or conditional orders are executed in essentially the same way. Since they are resting orders, however, they are not filled immediately. Rather, they are brought in to the pit and given to the pit broker who keeps them in his "deck." The deck consists of small cards on which the pit broker keeps track of orders he or she has filled, and the orders he or she needs to fill. Now let's take a look at the different types of orders that are possible and some of the intricacies that may be involved with some of these orders.

MARKET ORDER

A market order does exactly what it says. Placing an order to buy or sell at the market means that your order will be executed at the best possible price as soon as the pit broker has received it. In an active market, such orders are safe to use and very common. However, it is not prudent to use a market order in a less actively traded market and one should only be used if a fill is needed immediately.

In a slow market where the bids and offers are less frequent, a market order stands the chance of being filled far away from the last trade. If, for example, you place an order to buy at the market, but there are no price offers close to the last trade, the floor trader or pit broker will continue to bid higher and higher until your market order has been filled. In a thin or inactive market this could be at virtually any price. Therefore, your order will frequently not get filled at a very good price compared to what you think you should have gotten. Be very careful when using market orders in thin markets. In fact, it is best not to use market orders in such cases.

MARKET ON CLOSE (MOC) ORDERS

A market on close order is an instruction to the pit broker to execute an order for you, to buy or to sell at or near the close of trading. Your order is frequently executed during the last few seconds of trading and, in most cases, is not too much different than the closing price. Very frequently such orders are filled in the closing price range. On occasion, MOC orders do not result in particularly good fills. It has been my experience that MOC orders in most active markets do not result in terribly bad price fills. But several ticks difference between what you expected and what you received can occur.

On occasion, an MOC order will work to your advantage. This is particularly true when a market is near limit up or limit down. Assume, for an example, that you would like to buy at the end of the day. Assume that the market is weak. In such a case, the market will often drop even lower on the close as those who were buying during the day have MOC orders to sell. If you are short and have a MOC order to buy, or if you want to go net long, chances are you will get a reasonably good fill, often at or close to limit down.

The reverse often holds true with MOC orders to sell. In other words, if the market is sharply higher and you have a long position you would like to liquidate by the close, or a short you would like to establish, this could be an ideal situation. Frequently in a market that has been strong all day, there will be a rush to the upside bringing prices close to or possibly limit up. This happens because those who were short for the day rush in to cover their short positions. There will be buying, which runs the price up. Since you will be selling, you may get a better price fill than you expected. MOC orders should also be avoided in thin markets.

MARKET "NOT HELD"

This is an instruction to the floor broker to fill your order as best as he or she can and that you will not hold the pit broker accountable in the event of a poor fill. Such orders are generally not used by the public or for small amounts of contracts. Don't trouble the pit broker with such an order unless you have a large number of contracts to buy or sell.

MARKET ON THE OPEN ORDER

This is a very simple, self-explanatory order, entered before the opening to buy at the market as soon as the market opens. Typically, there is a great deal of activity on market opens, but in thin markets this could result in a reasonably bad price fill. Some market analysts and advisors have strong sentiment against buying on the open. They feel that the opening is not necessarily a good reflection of market activity. Indeed, on many occasions in the past, traders have witnessed significant reversals after a strong opening in a given direction.

Certainly, if our market entry was on the buy side on a sharply higher opening during one of the reversal type days, then we would indeed be in jeopardy, or vice versa during a sharply lower opening. However as I will demonstrate to you in a later chapter, the opening price in all markets is very important and I have developed a specific technique for using opening prices as a means of predicting significant levels of support and resistance.

STOP ORDERS

There are a number of stop orders. Stop orders are those which are generally either above or below the market. They are:

Buy Stop

This is an order to buy at a given price above the market. When the indicated price is hit, your order becomes a market order and it is filled at the best price possible thereafter. Such orders are used to exit a short position or to enter a long position on market strength.

Sell Stop

This is an order to sell at a price below the market. Once the price is hit, your order is filled at that price or at the best price possible. Such orders are used to exit a long position or to enter a short position on market weakness.

Stop Loss

The term "stop loss" is applied to a position that offsets an existing position. Such an order is designed to limit a loss, hence the name "stop loss." Orders are not entered as stop loss orders, but rather in the variety of ways described below. Hence, the term "stop loss" is a generic term that could be applied to orders above or below the market.

Stop Limit

The stop limit order is a specific type of stop order used either above or below the market. A sell stop limit means that you want to sell below the market, but at no lower than the price of your limit. In other words, you must be filled at your price or not at all. This is a good way to guarantee a fill at a certain price, but if the market goes through your price and does not trade at it, or the order cannot be filled even at the limit price, you will not be filled. You may not get the protection you want if you are using this as a stop loss. The reverse holds true for stop limit orders above the market.

Stop limits should be used when you want to avoid a bad fill, or when you are working with a precise technical level. I do not recommend using stop limits for the purpose of stop losses.

Stop Close Only

This is an instruction to sell or buy within the closing minute of trading. A sell stop close only order will be executed at or below the given price during the closing minute. A buy stop close only will be executed at or above the given price during the last minute of trading. Many times the fill price will not be in agreement with the last tick or settlement price due to the time span during which a stop close only order can be filled.

Fill or Kill Order

This order is not used very frequently; however, it has its merits. A fill or kill order is essentially an instruction to the pit broker to fill your order at a given price within a matter of minutes or to cancel your order. It is a way of placing a price order close to the market in an effort to obtain close to an immediate feedback on disposition of your order.

Such an order is best used when you wish to enter or exit a position quickly, but rather than doing so at the market you want to do so at a given price in order to avoid the possibility of a poor price fill. Fill or kill orders can be used in thin markets, or in markets that have been hovering around a certain price level but for some reason will not come to the price level at which you are seeking to enter or exit a position.

Good Till Canceled Orders

A good till canceled order means just that. An order is in the market until you cancel it. As a matter of procedure, most brokerage firms clear the books of orders at the end of every day's trading unless these orders are specified as good till canceled orders.

Most short-term traders do not find it necessary to use good till canceled orders. They can be used when you will be out of touch with the market, but I strongly suggest against trading when you are not in touch with the markets. Therefore, you will not need to use a good till canceled order. Such orders are much more common in the stock market.

SUMMARY

Price orders are very important inasmuch as they will affect the price at which you buy or sell. Naturally, this will also affect your bottom line. One thing to remember with regard to order placement is that you must be specific and decisive. Don't get a bad reputation with your broker by being unclear—saying one thing, but meaning another.

Finally, remember that in many cases existing orders must be found in the pit broker's deck before you can replace them with another order! This could markedly affect your price fill. Therefore, if you have an existing order that must be canceled and replaced with a market order, remember that your existing order will need to be found and removed so that there is no duplication. This takes time. The result could be a poor price fill. Therefore, if you suspect you will need to cancel and replace, cancel as soon as you can. Then enter your market order when ready. This will make certain your order is filled immediately and your resulting price fill could be better. Remember the cancel procedure. It could save you much grief and much money as well.

Part

4

Advanced Trading Strategies and Techniques

Chapter

14

Advanced Concepts in Moving Averages

My earlier discussion of moving averages illustrated the very basic applications and timing indicators of this technique. In recent years, the availability of high-powered computers at reasonably low prices has spawned many variations on the theme of moving averages. I have worked extensively with moving averages of highs and lows as opposed to moving averages of closing prices, and have found this technique exceptionally good at isolating support and resistance levels, as well as possible turning points in the markets.

For those who wish to pursue more advanced applications of the moving average techniques, I offer this chapter, which contains two moving average techniques. They both appear to have good potential as trading systems, but they are not offered here as such since specific money-management rules and stop-loss procedures would need to be added to the basic timing signals. Those who wish to develop these as trading systems should do more research on stop and risk procedures.

Chapter 14

THE MOVING AVERAGE CHANNEL (MAC)

The Moving Average Channel (MAC) is a concept developed by Richard Donchian in the 1950s. Instead of plotting just the moving average of closing prices, or for that matter of several closing prices, Donchian suggested plotting the moving averages of high and low prices of each time unit. The result was a price channel or band containing two moving averages, one of highs and one of lows.

I have found the technique to be especially interesting and have researched its possible applications. I found, for example, that the channel can work very well for the purpose of finding support and resistance. The MAC acts as support when prices decline in a bull market and as resistance when prices rally in a bear market. Figures 14–1, 14–2, and 14–3 show the channel, the channel with price, and various rallies to resistance and declines to support in established bull and bear markets.

The application of this technique is straightforward in terms of finding support and resistance. However, my work strongly suggests that more specific applications could be developed in terms of timing. Note the following characteristics of the moving average channel:

1. The moving average channel of ten units of the high and eight units of the low appears to be the most practical. Others are either too short or too long.

2. When a market has started a bullish move, corrections within that move tend to find support at either extreme of the channel or within the channel (i.e., price above channel).

3. In a bearish move, rallies tend to find resistance at either extreme of the channel or within the channel itself (i.e., price below channel).

4. Once price bars begin to appear fully outside of the channel on the upside, it is probable that a bullish move has started.

FIGURE 14-1   MOVING AVERAGE CHANNEL
(Reprinted with permission of Commodity Quote Graphics)

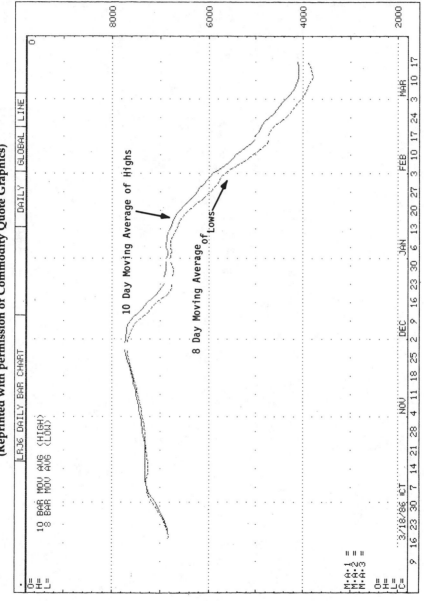

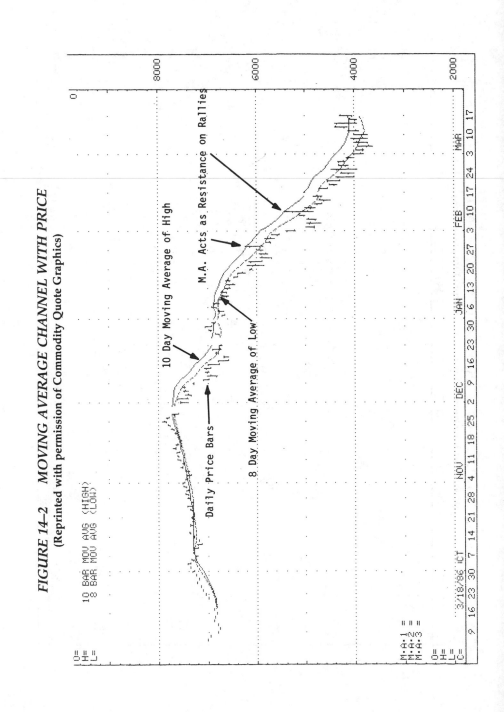

FIGURE 14-2   MOVING AVERAGE CHANNEL WITH PRICE
(Reprinted with permission of Commodity Quote Graphics)

FIGURE 14–3   MOVING AVERAGE CHANNEL WITH VARIOUS RALLIES
(Reprinted with permission of Commodity Quote Graphics)

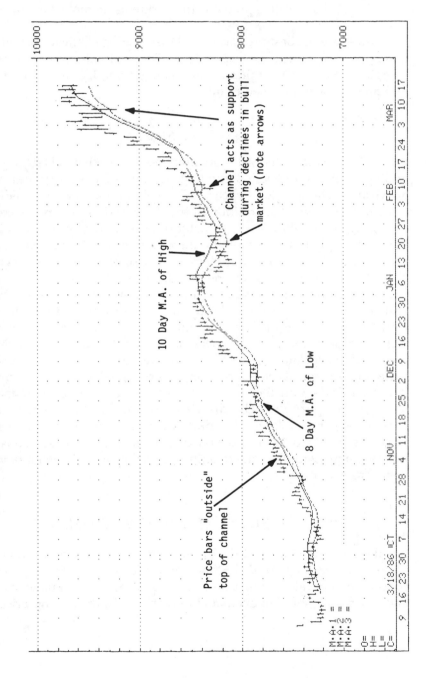

5. Once price bars begin to appear fully outside the bottom of
    the channel, it is probable that a downside move has started.

These are the basic applications I discovered. I believe they have
good potential value for the speculator. They help him or her to form
an opinion as to whether prices have changed trend, or if they remain
in a previously established trend.

One More Step

If we take one more step with the moving average channel technique,
adding to it a three-period moving average of closing prices, we
arrive at a technique that appears to have great potential as a trading
system. Essentially, the addition of the three-period moving average
of closing prices allows you to determine numerically when prices
have seemingly lost their momentum within the existing channel and
are likely to change direction. This is a way of determining when the
market has run out of gas on the upside or downside.

Figure 14–4 illustrates this technique, showing the potential buy
and sell signals using the indicator and relating these to an actual
price chart showing the hypothetical buy and sell points. Since the
technique determines when prices have probably turned higher or
lower, the speculator capable of assuming larger risk can use this
system in a reversal sense, following every signal, being in the market at all times, and thereby employing this technique for money-
management purposes. The drawback would be that losses could
sometimes get very large. Yet, profits would, at times, also be very
large. Figures 14–5, 14–6, and 14–7 offer some further illustrations of
this technique with the understanding that they are still being developed as a trading system.

MOVING AVERAGE TRADING BAND (MATB)

Another, and most interesting, application of the moving average is
its use as a trading band. Recent applications of the trading-band
concept incorporate closing prices and a percentage price band above
and beyond the moving average. In other words, the closing price is

FIGURE 14-4 **TEN-DAY HIGH/EIGHT-DAY LOW CHANNEL WITH THREE-DAY CLOSE MOVING AVER-AGES AND HYPOTHETICAL TIMING SIGNALS**
(Reprinted with permission of Commodity Quote Graphics)

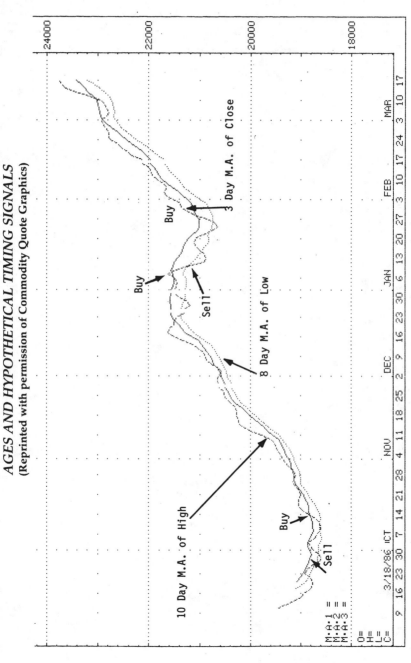

FIGURE 14-5   TEN-DAY HIGH/EIGHT-DAY LOW/THREE-DAY CLOSE M.A. CHANNEL SIGNALS
(B = BUY, S = SELL)

(Reprinted with permission of Commodity Quote Graphics)

FIGURE 14–6 TEN-DAY HIGH/EIGHT-DAY LOW/THREE-DAY CLOSE M.A. CHANNEL SIGNALS
(B = BUY, S = SELL)

(Reprinted with permission of Commodity Quote Graphics)

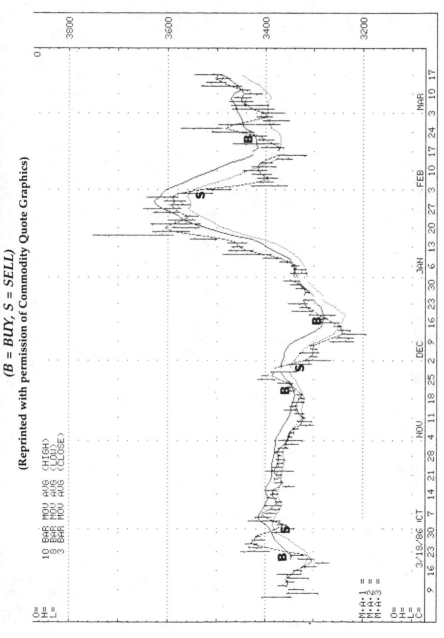

*FIGURE 14-7   TEN-DAY HIGH/EIGHT-DAY LOW/THREE-DAY CLOSE M.A. CHANNEL AND TIMING
SIGNALS (B = BUY, S = SELL)—HOURLY CHART*
(Reprinted with permission of Commodity Quote Graphics)

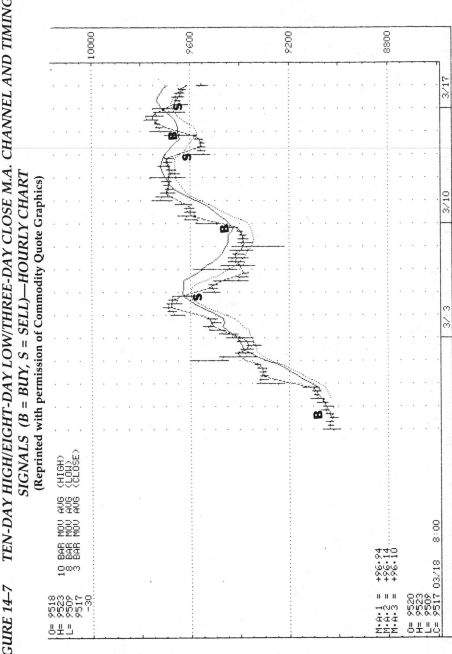

used to determine a given moving average, and a percentage band above and below the closing price is constructed as a timing band within which prices tend to move back and forth as they form support and resistance usually at upper and lower ends of the channel.

Figures 14–8 and 14–9 illustrate two markets using a band of prices above and below the moving average. In this case, I have employed a moving average of five days and a channel of 1.5 percent above the closing price and 0.7 percent below the closing price. The concept illustrated here is fairly simple. Essentially, it suggests that the upper end of the channel tends to serve as resistance and the lower end of the channel or band tends to serve as support. I have indicated by arrows the examples of these levels. For many years I have considered the opening price to be rather important. This runs contrary to the teachings of many traders, who feel that market openings should not be used for establishing positions. There is a subtle difference between my approach and theirs. While I am not disputing the possibility that bad price fills may be obtained by trading on the opening, I am saying that the opening price is, nonetheless, important and that it can be valuable in technical work.

Reconstructing the MATB using opening price as the determinant of moving average, let's examine Figures 14–10 and 14–11. Note the results. What is most intriguing to me about using the moving average of opening prices is the fact that the opening price is known early in each day's trading session. The MATS of opening prices is known when the markets open. Speculators could use the opening price as a means of calculating the MATS in order to forecast possible buy and sell points at support and resistance for use during the current day.

Consider the MATS in relation to the typical moving average work being done by most market technicians. I have also included two charts (Figures 14-12 and 14-13) showing the MATS on intraday charts.

Simple Moving Average

The simple moving average is calculated by adding and then averaging a set of prices or other data which spans a specific amount of time. The calculation normally involves closing prices, but may also

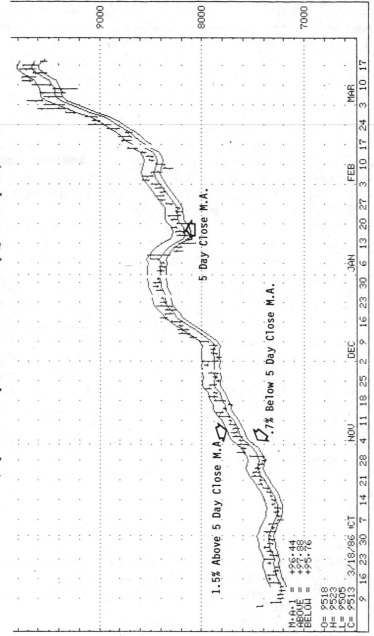

FIGURE 14-8 FIVE-DAY CLOSE M.A. AND BAND
(Reprinted with permission of Commodity Quote Graphics)

FIGURE 14-9   FIVE-DAY CLOSE M.A. AND BAND
(Reprinted with permission of Commodity Quote Graphics)

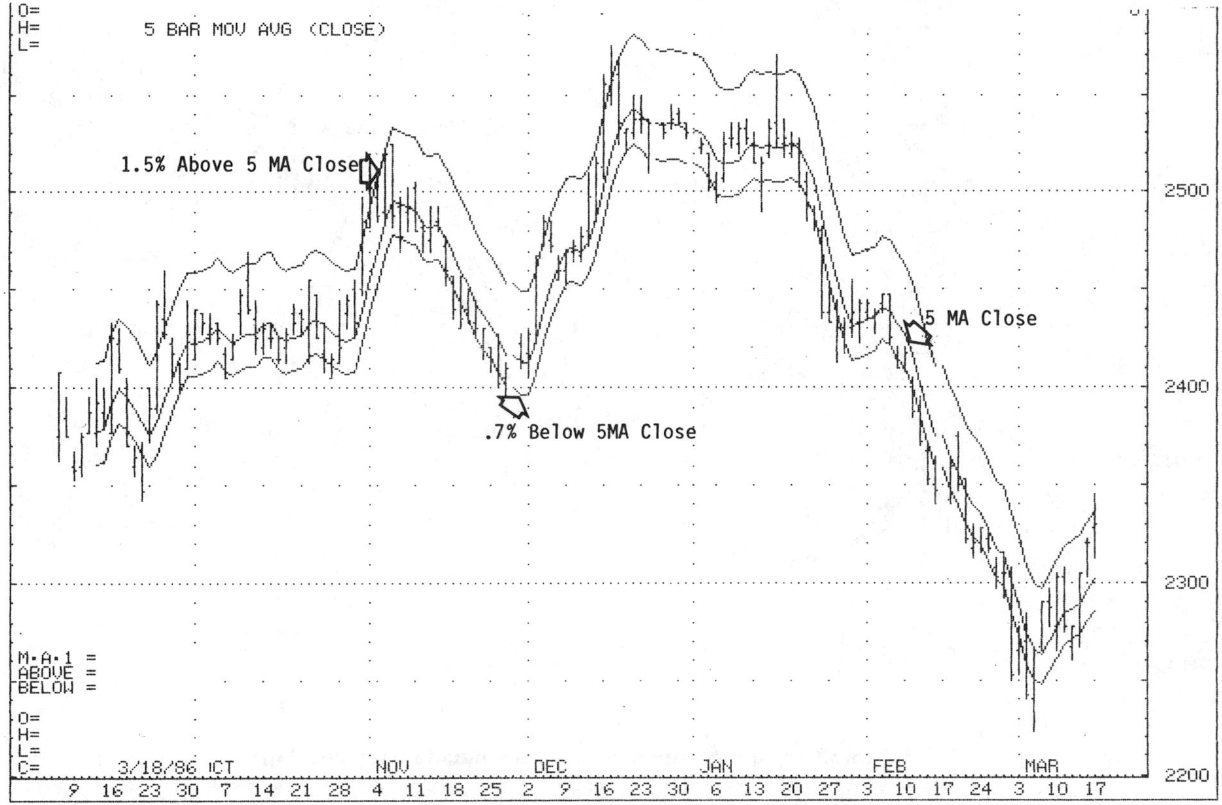

FIGURE 14–10 MOVING AVERAGE CHANNEL OPENING BAND
(Reprinted with permission of Commodity Quote Graphics)

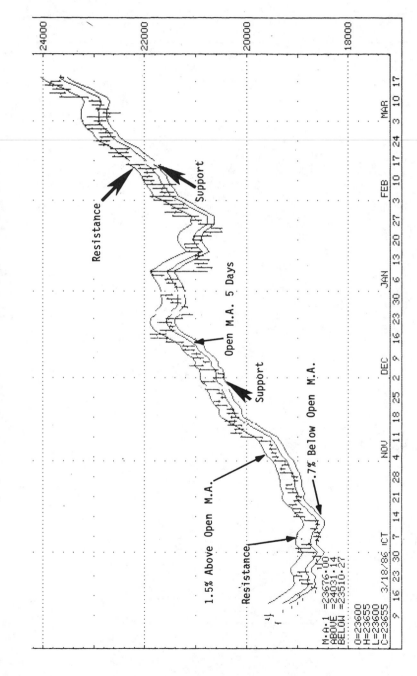

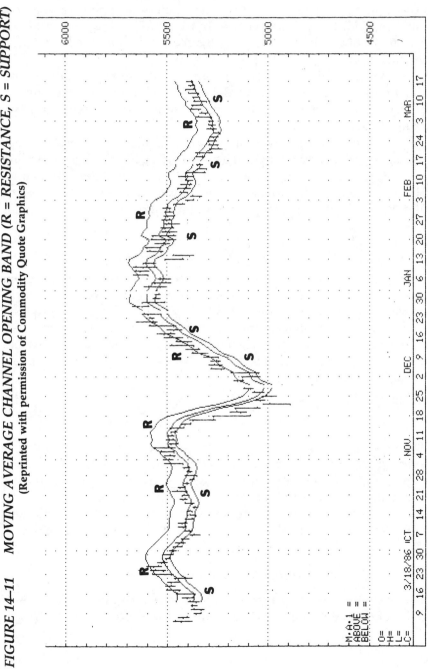

FIGURE 14–11   MOVING AVERAGE CHANNEL OPENING BAND (R = RESISTANCE, S = SUPPORT)
(Reprinted with permission of Commodity Quote Graphics)

be calculated from highs, lows, or an average of all three, or from other numerical data. The oldest data point is dropped when a new one is added. Hence, the average "moves" following the market. A line graph of the daily averages will appear as a smoothed version of the raw data.

Longer moving averages smooth out all minor fluctuations and show only longer-term trends. Conversely, shorter-term moving averages will accentuate the short-term trends at the expense of long-term trends.

Long-term and short-term moving averages each have their advantages and disadvantages. In general, using a longer-term moving average will allow you to enter and exit the market less frequently. Shorter-term averages are used to quickly enter and exit the markets, and do not capture the major trend of a market.

Weighted Moving Average

A weighted moving average places greater emphasis on more recent data by weighting each day's data differently. Whereas the simple moving average gives equal weight to each data point, the weighted moving average assigns more importance to recent data. Some traders claim that recent prices are more important than older prices and prefer to use the weighted moving average since it tends to react quickly to recent data.

Exponential Moving Averages

The exponential moving average is similar to the weighted moving average in that it assigns greater importance to more recent data. However, the exponential moving average continues to take into account all of the data points. Both exponential and weighted moving averages tend to generate more trades in tight, trading range markets which can result in costly whipsaws (i.e., numerous false signals).

Triangular Moving Averages

The triangular moving average assigns greater importance to midpoint of the data series. Consequently it is less affected by old prices

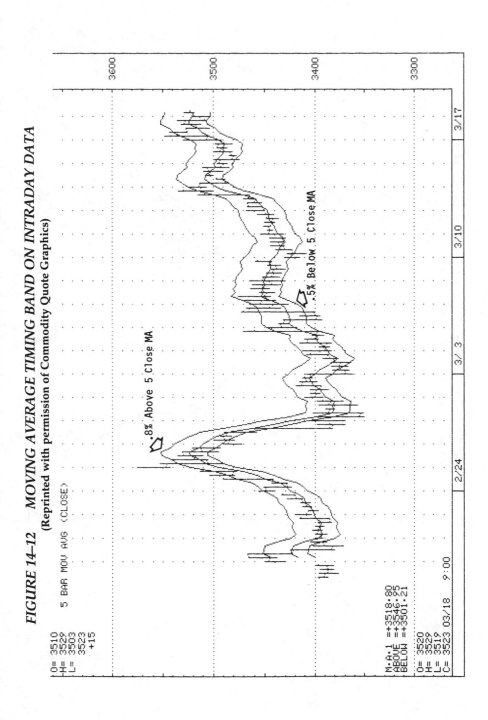

FIGURE 14-12 MOVING AVERAGE TIMING BAND ON INTRADAY DATA
(Reprinted with permission of Commodity Quote Graphics)

FIGURE 14–13   MOVING AVERAGE TIMING BAND ON INTRADAY DATA
(Reprinted with permission of Commodity Quote Graphics)

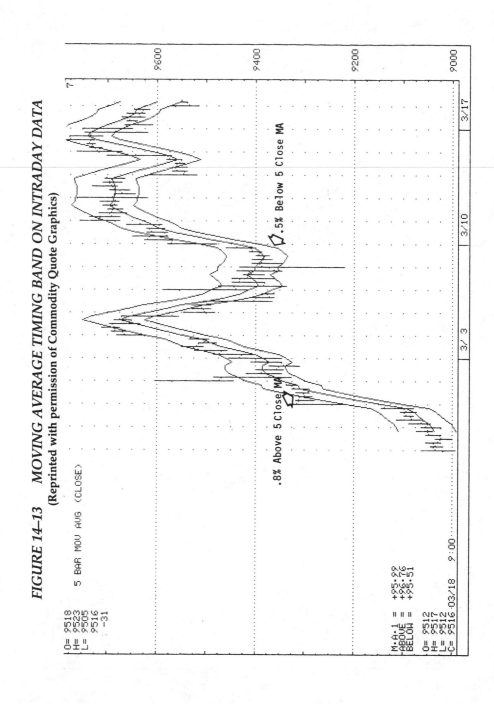

and new prices. Research indicates that triangular moving averages are more stable than either weighted or exponential moving averages.

Best Performing Moving Averages

In order to examine the performance of moving averages, I conducted an exhaustive test of numerous dual and triple moving averages. Some combinations were considerably better than others but all moving averages were subject to large drawdowns and required large risk. The results are discussed in my book, *Strategic Futures Trading* (1992).[1]

SUMMARY

Several basic moving averages and their methods were discussed. A synopsis of the advantages and limitations of different moving averages were described. Particularly intriguing is the technique that employs opening prices, since opening prices are known early in the trading session, and can be employed in a predictive fashion for the purpose of establishing support and resistance.

---

1   Bernstein, Jacob, *Strategic Futures Trading,* Chicago: Dearborn Financial Publishing, 1992.

Chapter

15

Aspects of Intraday Trading

For many years, futures traders and aspiring futures traders have been cautioned against the "evils of day trading." The public has been told that profitable day trading is impossible unless you are a professional, a floor trader, or a speculator who is paying minimal commissions. Though it may have been true in the past that day trading was an art reserved only for the select few, a number of changes within the futures industry, as well as in the area of market technology, have significantly altered this situation.

Discount brokerage became popular in the 1980s, and the ensuing commission price war caused rates to fall precipitously. The competition has been fierce in the industry, but beneficial to the consumer. It has certainly taken its toll within the futures brokerage community.

Nonetheless, it now appears to me that the services many discount brokers provide are often equal to or better than what is true for many full-service firms. In view of the trend toward lower commission rates, increased computer power, and the rapid communications now possible between the public speculator and the floor of the trading exchanges, intraday trading has become more of a reality for all types of traders. The dangers of intraday trading are no longer valid today. In fact, it may be more fruitful to consider the possible benefits that may be derived from short-term trading.

Consider my list. It is not designed to influence you into making short-term or intraday trading your main focus, but rather to give you a different perspective from what you may have been exposed to in the past.

POSSIBLE ADVANTAGES OF INTRADAY TRADING

1. More efficient use of margin money.

2. Ability to test trading systems more rapidly in real time.

3. Intraday traders will need to do less market analysis, since they are not concerned with major price trends.

4. Intraday traders generally do not need to know the news since any intraday news will have an immediate impact on the market, thereby changing technical indicators, which, if reasonably good, will permit a capitalization on the trend change.

5. Intraday traders will be out of their positions at the end of the day—win, lose, or draw. An intraday trader who does not do so is not an intraday trader. Therefore, you will be forced to take your losses quickly, overcoming an obstacle that proves to be the undoing of many position traders (i.e., riding losses).

6. There are many good intraday price swings, particularly in the more active markets. This means there is profit potential.

7. You will be forced to have discipline. Intraday trading requires the utmost discipline. It will be a good proving ground for you. Even if you choose not to do intraday trad-

ing consistently, the experience and the lessons learned will be valuable in all types of trading and investing.

8. You will obtain a fresh start each day. By starting fresh each day you will not be concerned about a loss or profit you may be riding from the previous day. The start of each new day is the start of a new relationship with the market, and with it a new opportunity.

9. You need not trade every day. Intraday traders can call it quits at the end of each day. Consequently, you can leave for trips, vacations, or other business any time you choose. You will not need to be concerned about a position you may have, and you will not need to be concerned about positions you may want to take.

There are probably many other potential advantages to intraday trading. Though this book is not intended to be a treatise in support of intraday trading, you may want to consider some of these advantages in your overall decision regarding the markets.

Certainly there are some prerequisites to intraday trading that must be met before a decision is made. Some of these have been discussed earlier in this book, but permit me to reiterate them as the major issues facing the individual who is about to make or has already made a decision to trade on an intraday basis. I would say that if you have any doubts about fulfilling all the following prerequisites, then you ought not consider intraday trading.

PREREQUISITES TO INTRADAY TRADING

1. **Time**
    You must be able to make a time commitment. You must watch the market actively all day or until your positions have been closed out. You cannot do other things while trading intraday. You need not trade intraday every day of the week, but for those days that you do trade intraday, your total attention will be required.

2. **Quotes**
   In order to trade actively intraday, you will need one or all of the above. Some individuals believe they can trade intraday using quotations obtained from television shows, radio talk commodity futures programs, or quotes from their broker. While it is possible to trade short term with limited information, intraday trading is either difficult or impossible if you do not have access to the above. While a computer may not be necessary, you must have a method that is simple to calculate, permitting prompt decision-making.

   Note that a quotation system is not absolutely necessary with certain trading systems. There are some systems which generate buy and sell points based on the previous day's trading range, and which enter on buy or sell stops the next day. These systems also use specific stop losses and, therefore, allow all orders to be entered before the market opens. Hence, a quotation system is not necessary in such cases.

3. **Low Commissions**
   Use a broker who charges you reasonably low commissions. As I explained earlier, the cost of commissions is a major one for the day trader. You must keep this cost as low as possible, while retaining good price fills.

4. **Prompt Order Executions**
   Frequently, you may be in and out of day trade positions within a matter of minutes. If you should wish to exit a position within a matter of minutes after you entered, you will need to know the price at which you entered. If you do not know, then the delay of obtaining this information may prove costly. This is why it is very important to trade with a brokerage firm that can provide you with prompt reporting of order fills.

5. **Discipline**
   I have already discussed the issue of discipline in this book. I won't bother to underscore its importance in a day trading

program. I refer you to previous chapters and sections that deal with the subject.

6. **A Trading System or Method**
    You will need a system that will alert you to intraday moves very early in their inceptions.

These are some of the prerequisites to day trading. If you are currently day trading and find that your results are not what they should be, or if you are considering day trading, I urge you strongly to consider them carefully.

OTHER ASPECTS OF INTRADAY TRADING

An important issue to consider with intraday trading is the aspect of stop losses versus price objectives. The day trader must make decisions as to whether a position should be closed out once it reaches a certain profit objective, or whether a stop loss should be employed in the event that the position turns against the trader.

It is not an uncommon experience to have a position work in one's favor for a period of time, and then turn against one without a concomitant trading signal to change positions. On occasion, this will result in the profit being lost, while on other occasions the profit might actually turn into a loss. This is an unacceptable situation for the day trader, since profits must be closely guarded in order to preserve trading profitability on the bottom line. Two approaches can be used to solve this dilemma, each with its positive and negative aspects.

USING OBJECTIVES

One approach is to employ specific objectives for each market. In Treasury bonds, for instance, one might set an objective of 10 points. (This is merely an illustration. The 10-point objective is not something I have determined through research.) Every time the market allows you the opportunity to take a 10-point profit or greater, you will take it. Unfortunately, the speculator who practices this approach may leave considerable profit in the market, should the position continue to move in the anticipated direction. Many times there are very large intraday moves and the practice of taking a 10-point profit will not only limit profits, but will also cause the speculator to lose his or her position. There may not be an opportunity to re-enter the market later in the day for participation in continued moves.

On the other hand, the market may reverse direction and the speculator would be thankful that the 10-point profit was taken. Unfortunately, there is no definitive way to know in advance what to do and when to do it. Therefore, an alternative procedure might be advisable.

TRAILING STOPS

There have been ongoing arguments both in favor of and opposed to trailing stops. Most of these discussions have been related to the use of stops for position trades. While it may be true that a trailing stop for position trades might not be an effective procedure, I maintain that a trailing stop should, indeed, be used for a day trade once a given profit objective has been attained. In other words, I recommend that once you have reached a certain profit level for each day trade (in dollar terms), you enter a stop loss that will pay your commissions and eliminate or greatly reduce the possibility of your profit turning into a loss. This will help avoid one of the worst situations for a day trader allowing a profit to turn into a loss.

Furthermore, by a series of predetermined steps, the stop loss should be continually raised, closer and closer to the existing market price, so that as the day's end approaches, the possibility of locking in a profit is increased. Naturally, a level will be reached where it is irrational to place a stop loss and more advantageous to simply liquidate the position at the market.

SYSTEMS AND METHODS

The popularity of day trading and short-term trading is evidenced by the number of short-term trading systems that are available to the public. There are many different techniques for day trading, some employing black box systems whose details are not known to the user. Other technical systems are available in the form of written computer software. Still other systems are less computerized or not computerized at all.

It is difficult to say which system or systems are best suited for use by any particular individual, since there are so many from which to choose and there are so many different objectives and expectations when it comes to intraday trading. Hopefully I can give you some guidelines and suggestions as to a few viable techniques.

"THE OLD STANDBYS"

Some of the traditional technical approaches described in this book are applicable to intraday trading. With the exception of the fact that all positions must be closed out by the end of the day's trading, the entry techniques discussed in this book are all reasonable methods. The exit techniques of such systems as moving averages, the moving average channel method, the moving average band method, traditional chart patterns, and timing signal analysis are also viable. Futures traders, however, like all consumers, are always searching for the new and better, and in this search new products are constantly being developed for use by day traders.

Stop and consider, however, that the professional day trader on the floor of the exchange does not generally have access to a computer and must keep track of most technical work mentally or must trade on the basis of gut feel. I certainly have nothing against trading on the basis of gut feel or intuition, as long as it is successful. Most individuals, however, cannot do this and, therefore, even trading in the pit requires some sort of a systematic approach, even if it is not as mechanical as might be desired.

As an addition to the standard techniques I have already described, all of which, to varying degrees can be applied to day trading, let me suggest to you an approach which until recently has not been especially practical since it requires constant monitoring of prices. It is, however, an approach for any individual who is in close touch with the markets.

The "tick chart" employs a very elementary concept. It is as elementary to use as it is to maintain. Yet, in its simplicity, it is highly complex since it represents a number of significant technical aspects of the market. The tick chart is, very simply, a price chart that records in dot fashion all prices at which a market trades during a given period of time. In other words, if one were recording a tick chart on gold futures using five-minute increments of time, one would simply place a dot (or some other distinguishing mark) at the appropriate coordinates on the chart in order to illustrate that the market had traded at that price.

That price, whatever it might have been, has already been "ticked at" and will not be recorded again. If the market were to continue to trade at that price, or if the market did not trade at all subsequent to this for the remainder of the five minutes, no other marks would be recorded in the five-minute time segment. When the five-minute segment ends, the next five-minute segment is started and a mark is placed at the next price tick. Assume that the market then ticks at a higher price. A tick is placed at that price. Assume then that the market ticks up again. A tick is placed in that price, and so on.

The method sounds simple enough. Yet, in its simplicity, it is most revealing. The tick chart allows the trader to determine levels of support, resistance, accumulation, distribution, breaks of resistance, and breaks of support. By letting the trader know where and when considerable trading took place, the trader can have a good idea of where and when prices could find support on declines or resistance on rallies. The assumption is that if prices traded for a relatively long time within a given price range, then this level will likely serve as one of support when prices ultimately decline. Some of the other technical ramifications will be illustrated later on (see Figures 15–1 to 15–3).

The tick chart can be maintained on time frames of the user's choice. The shorter the time frame, the more active the trading signals generated by the tick chart will be. Furthermore, certain forms of traditional analysis can be applied to the tick chart as means of generating additional signals.

In addition to the techniques described in this book, there are many other approaches, systems, methods, and techniques to day trading. There are probably hundreds of different approaches, all of which may have potential, provided the basic rules of money management and sensibility are adhered to.

FIGURE 15–1   FIVE-MINUTE INTRADAY TICK CHART
(Reprinted with permission of Commodity Quote Graphics)

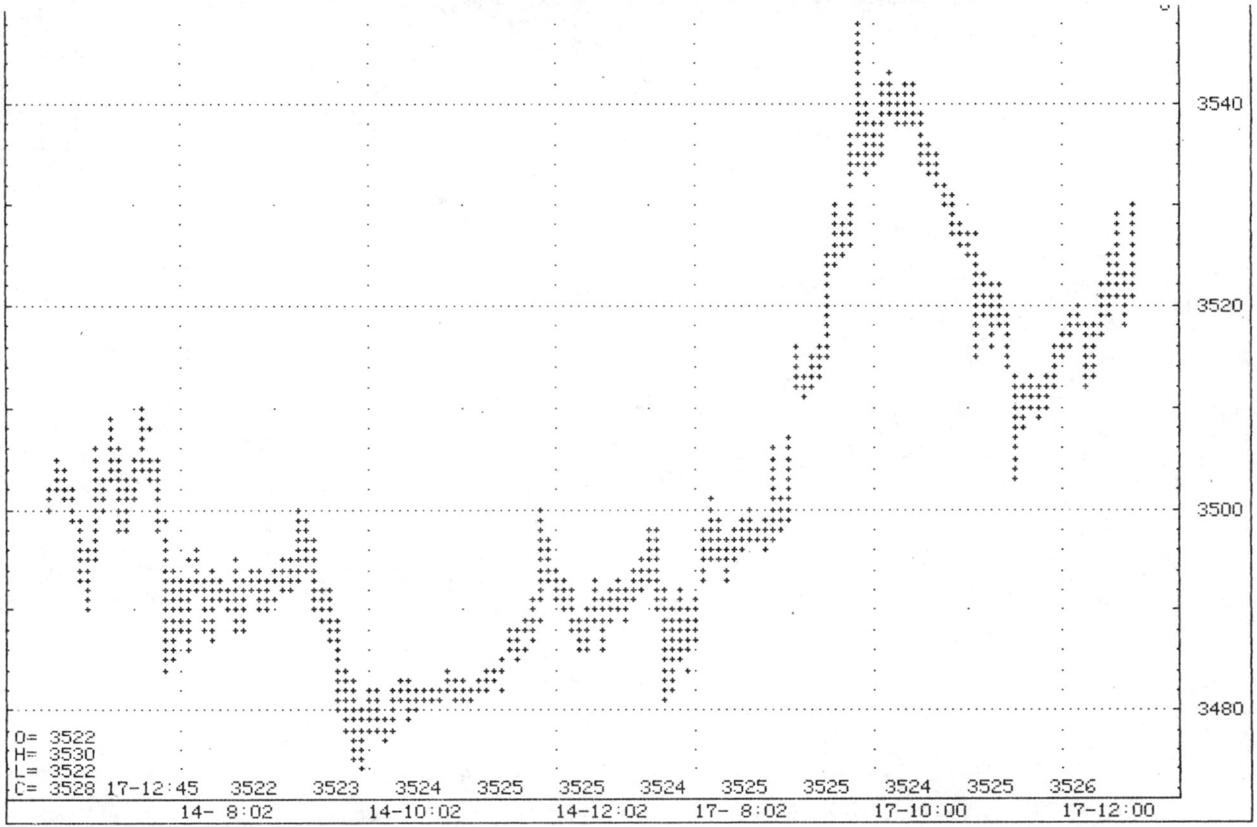

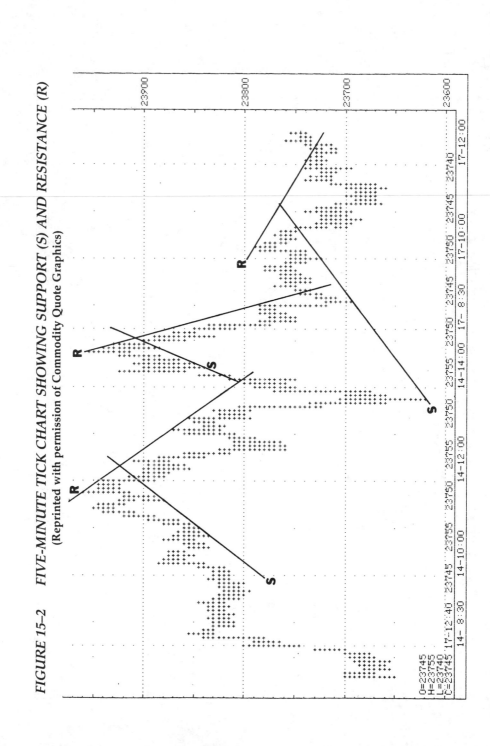

FIGURE 15–2   FIVE-MINUTE TICK CHART SHOWING SUPPORT (S) AND RESISTANCE (R)
(Reprinted with permission of Commodity Quote Graphics)

FIGURE 15-3   TICK CHART SHOWING SUPPORT (S) AND RESISTANCE(R)
(Reprinted with permission of Commodity Quote Graphics)

I can certainly say that with respect to intraday trading, discipline is more important than it is with any other approach. Yet, day trading has a built in disciplinarian, if you will, in the sense that the day trader must be out of his or her position at the end of the day if truly committed to day trading. I would say that with very few exceptions (probably fewer than five in 100) positions should never be kept overnight if you are strict about your day trading approach. All too often, those who do keep day trades overnight are rather disappointed they did so when the next day's trading begins.

This is not to say that significant amounts of money cannot be made by maintaining a position overnight, particularly in recent years, when opening price gaps have been particularly large. However, since the name of the day trading game is to reduce risk, why increase it by holding positions overnight?

SUMMARY

This chapter advanced the notion that intraday trading may not necessarily be the evil that so many have for so many years reported it to be. I outlined my reasons in favor of intraday trading, illustrated some intraday trading techniques, and also discussed the prerequisites of intraday trading.

Chapter

16

Futures Options: Are They for You?

A more recent addition to the world of speculation is the futures option contract. Just as traders were beginning to understand stock indices, interest rate futures, and currencies futures, along comes the futures options market to confuse the issue. It was rather ironic that futures options were unleashed upon the public during a period of time (1985-1986) that has been very difficult for many traders. Perhaps the rationale by those who have been planning futures options was to provide a vehicle to the public by which maximum loss would be the cost of the option plus commission.

To fully understand how options can be used and abused in futures trading, let's examine some very simple definitions of the futures options contract, and some elementary applications of these vehicles. Let me stress at the outset that this chapter cannot provide a comprehensive analysis and explanation of the literally hundreds of possible uses of futures options. Interested parties should consult some of the recent texts on this subject. The discussion that follows should be sufficient to get you started in the right direction.

TWICE REMOVED

Futures options are very difficult for the average individual to understand because they deal with a "twice-removed" abstract concept. Stock options are simple to understand because they relate to an underlying security or a relatively tangible asset (i.e., shares of stock, which represent ownership of an entity). An option on a future is, in effect, an intangible on top of an intangible. Since a futures contract often represents something that has not yet been produced or manufactured, an option to buy or sell something that is not yet real is even more abstract to the general public.

Yet, the concept should not be so unfamiliar, since many areas of the investor's world currently deal in fairly similar abstracts. Options on new construction are a good example. A builder begins to develop a piece of property for apartments or condominiums. In order to sell the units, the builder sells options to buy units that have not yet been constructed. The option gives a buyer the right to purchase one of the units by a certain date. Sale of the option raises cash for the builder and locks in the buyer's right to purchase a unit (usually at a fixed price) at some point in the future, regardless of what prices may have risen to or fallen to by that time. The buyer of the real-estate option can apply the purchase price toward the purchase of the unit at contract closing.

In many ways, the futures option is similar, but the buyer won't necessarily get his or her money back when the contract expires. A futures option gives the buyer of the option the right to buy or sell the underlying futures contract at a given price at some time in the future, regardless what the actual price may be. Therefore, if a buyer of an option is fortunate, or better yet, has done good technical research or exercised good judgment, and the underlying market moves in his or her favor, the option will increase in value, since the underlying futures contract will increase in value.

The creators of futures options, in their great wisdom and foresight, have given us two types of options. The call option gives the buyer the right to buy the underlying futures contract by a certain date at a certain price regardless of the actual price. The put option gives its buyer the right to sell the futures contract at a certain price at some point in the future regardless of what the actual price may be. You can readily see that if you buy a call option and the price of the underlying commodity goes up, you make money. If you buy a put option and the price of the underlying commodity goes down you also make money. There is certainly no more mystery to this than being long or short the market.

MANY WAYS TO GO

Imagine the myriad possibilities that are feasible when futures and options are employed in conjunction. The many different combinations or strategies include such things as buying a call option and selling a call option of a different month, buying a call option and buying a put option at the same time, buying the underlying commodity and buying the put option to protect yourself, buying call options instead of the underlying commodity to minimize risk, buying put options instead of the underlying commodity to minimize risk, and so on. There are numerous combinations of the above.

Is it no wonder then, that options and option strategies have proven overwhelming to most speculators. Due to such complexities, their reception into the world of futures trading has not been an especially smooth one, with the exception of options on Treasury bond futures. Primarily this poor reception has been a function of ignorance on the part of the public and its consequent unwillingness to accept futures options as a viable means of limiting risk.

ADVANTAGES OF FUTURES OPTIONS

The advertised advantage of futures options is the fact that their buyers have limited risk. Risk is limited to the cost of the option plus commission. In other words, if purchase of a futures options contract costs you $600, then the absolute maximum you can lose will be commission plus $600. Such limited loss factor has great appeal to the public and constitutes the primary marketing tool used to interest speculators in futures options.

A secondary benefit of options is the fact that they can increase tremendously on a percentage basis over a very short period of time. Couple this with specific limited loss and tremendous upside potential, and you have an almost ideal situation on which to sell a speculator.

Another benefit of futures options is that, up to a certain point, they will continue to hold their value and, as a consequence, they will buy you time without forcing you out of the market. If, for example, you expect gold to make a major move down, but you do not know for certain when the move will occur, you could buy a put option without being concerned that you must have precise timing on your entry. The put will buy you time and, within a reasonable time frame, you will be able to withstand moves in the market against you, knowing that your maximum loss is specifically limited. The only way you can lose is if the market continues to go against you or if the market goes nowhere.

This "buying time" feature is especially beneficial to an agricultural producer who may wish to hedge against crops by purchasing the appropriate put options. Since the market for many options is large and liquid, he could close out the option at any time. Naturally, however, the worst thing that can happen is that your option will become worthless and you will lose its entire value.

Another feature of options is that their value can be very accurately predicted at any time. Each option's value is clearly related to the underlying value of the futures contract it represents and its time to expiration. A considerable number of statistical computer programs are available in the field of options evaluation. These programs will allow you to evaluate various strategies over a specific period of time, using possible price objectives. They will give you the potential value of your option, given the outcome of each scenario. Institutional money managers, stock fund managers, and pension fund managers can employ options in stock index futures and Treasury bond futures, in programs to hedge against their holdings either in the cash markets and/or in stocks/mutual funds.

LIABILITIES AND LIMITATIONS OF FUTURES OPTIONS

The single greatest liability of futures options is that they provide speculators with a false sense of security. Whereas the producer may certainly benefit, the trading public or individual speculator frequently feels that there is less risk in entering an options position than might be the case in a futures contract. The speculator may be enticed out of making a trade in the net market, since he or she feels that an option will cost less and could yield more.

While it is true that the option may indeed cost less and could yield more, it appears just as difficult to make money speculating in options as it does speculating in futures. The logic of options seems to be irrefutable, but it must be fully understood that time is of the essence. The speculator reasons, "Why should I risk losing $1,600 in gold on a futures contract when I can buy a gold call option for $850, with the possibility that gold may rally several thousand dollars per contract?" The hope or expectation here is that the individual will have sufficient time to participate in at least a portion of the move. Had a position been taken in nothing but the futures contract, it is possible that the trader may not have been able to withstand a move in the opposite direction. But the option also had limited time.

The use of a limited-risk futures options strategy in conjunction with cyclic price tendencies is a very sensible strategy. The procedure is described at the end of this chapter in greater detail. Though options will limit your risk, you may take many more total losses due to deterioration of time value (called "time decay").

The attractiveness of futures options due to their limited risk and high profit potential can be illusory. The speculator should not only see the limited risk and high potential, but he or she should also be aware of the downside. If 20 option positions are taken with a loss of $400 on most, then the few winners must be large ones if the overall result is to be positive. Although you may be enamored of the obvious benefits in options, you should not lose sight of their probability of success when used in the typical fashion. Certainly, if this is your first venture into the futures trading area, and if you have very limited capital, then options may not be the right thing for you.

The specific manner in which you use futures options strategies is significantly more important than the underlying limited risk of these vehicles. As in the case of futures market transactions, you must attempt to use options in the same way that professionals do. This is not especially simple, but there are very specific methods and procedures for doing so.

As you can see, futures options are for you if you use them the right way. If, however, you are looking to make a killing by trading extremely low priced (i.e., out of the money) futures options, then your odds are not especially good. I will assume that you have some very general knowledge of options trading since my purpose in this book is not to cover the field of options from start to finish. The intent is, as I have expressed earlier, to give a very general overview that will ultimately provide you with direction and save you time. Remember, above all, that futures options trading is not a panacea for avoiding losses.

SOME SUGGESTED STRATEGIES

Here are some very elementary strategies that are feasible, but that, as you will see, have different applications. I suggest you consult a more thorough text for complete strategic methodology if you have a serious interest in futures options implementation.

1. **Buy a Call Option Instead of Going Long**.
    Assume that you have good reason to believe a market is going higher. You wish to limit your risk by using an option instead of buying the underlying futures contract. What should you do? Here are a few questions to consider. Do you expect a large move or a small one? Do you expect a short- or a long-term move? How much time should it take?

    Generally, if you expect a short-term move, then you might consider buying an in-the-money option, or an option that is near the money. In other words, an in-the-money option is one that trades above the strike price, whereas a near the money option is one that trades close to the strike price. Such options will be higher priced, but they will move at the same rate or at a greater rate than the underlying market.

An alternate procedure that involves lower risk would be to buy options that are farther from the money by virtue of their nearer expiration or larger distance from the strike price. Such options may be selling at much lower prices, but may only move one-third as quickly as the underlying contract. In order to answer these types of questions, it is best to use an options evaluation program, either one provided by a software service or one maintained by your brokerage house. You can get some very specific answers to these questions by running one of these programs.

2. **Buy Put Options in Expectation of a Down-Move**.
The procedure here would be essentially similar to what has been described for call options above, but you would buy puts instead of calls, expecting prices to move lower, and the puts to move up. The same general rules would apply.

3. **You Expect a Large Up-Move; Buy Futures and Buy Put Options for Protection**.
To a certain extent, this is a spread strategy. Assume that you expect a market to move much higher and you plan on purchasing, or you have already purchased a net long position in the futures market. Assume also that you wish to protect yourself from having a naked long position or assume you want to protect your call option. You could get some protection by buying a put option that would be limited in cost, but, in the event of a decline in your underlying long position, would protect you from significant loss.

Naturally, you would be liable for commissions on each, and if your net long position goes in your favor, the put option position will decrease in value. This, however, is not an especially bad strategy since there is no limit to how high the long futures contract may go, but the put option can only decrease to zero. If, for example, you establish a long position in soybeans expecting a 50-cent up-move (which would be worth $2,500 per contract) and you establish a long put option position (costing you $700), your potential would be $2,500 minus $700 worth of "insurance."

Assuming that the long soybeans went against you, your put option would increase in value, though not necessarily on a par with the decrease of your long position. The right combination of long futures and long put options is necessary to give you complete protection. Remember that "time decay" is your enemy.

4. **Sell Short Futures; Buy a Call for Protection**.
    This procedure works exactly the opposite way from the one just described. Again, the right fit or match of call options and short futures contracts is important for complete protection.

5. **You Expect a Major Move, but You Don't Know Which Way**.
    Some markets are notorious for making big moves. Treasury bond futures, for example, have made some major moves throughout the years. Yet there are times when you are not certain which way the move will go. Underlying market conditions such as bullish consensus, trading volume, economic factors, chart patterns, cycles, and volumes all suggest that the market is likely to make a large move. Still, you are not certain in which direction. You could purchase a put and a call on the same market, which would mean the only way you would come out at a loss is if this market fails to make a big move during the life span of your options.

6. **Covered Options Strategies Are Also Possible**.
    In such cases, you become the seller of a call or put option, taking in the money from the buyer and protecting yourself with a futures position that will cover you in the event of a move against you. These strategies are considerably safer, yet they may not yield as much as naked options sales.

7. **Differential in Long-Term, Short-Term, and Intermediate-Term Moves**.
   Many times, the market will move differently based on near-term and far-term expectations. A prime example is short-term and long-term interest rates. While there are times when short-term interest rates will decline with long-term interest rates holding steady, there may also be times during which long-term interest rates decline and short term rates actually go up. Such situations are ideal for spreading two ends against this middle or various combinations of spreads.

   Such spreads using futures options are numerous, and an entire science of spreading with its own lingo and methodology has evolved in recent years. The simple act of spreading near-term vs. long-term vs. mid-term rates is called a butterfly spread. In such an instance, a speculator might buy a nearby option, buy a deferred option, and sell two options in the middle. Such spreads can combine exceptionally low risk with tremendous profit potential, provided your timing and conceptualization of market conditions are correct. For those wishing to dig more deeply into this subject, there are many good references available.

SUMMARY

This overview clarified the doubly intangible nature of futures options. Many distinct strategies employing futures options were identified and later discussed, especially regarding their value in limiting speculators' and producers' risks. Readers were warned against the limitations inherent in trading futures options, including limited profit potential as compared to the underlying futures contracts. Time decay, or the rapid time deterioration of the options premium was mentioned as a severely negative factor.

Chapter

17

How to Develop Your Own Trading Plan

A common complaint I hear from many futures traders, both in the public and professional sectors, is that there is too much information to digest. There are numerous computerized trading systems, perhaps thousands of different trading techniques, and a wide variety of computer software programs and hardware combinations in addition to countless newsletter services, chart services, advisors, consultants, brokers, managed-account programs, guided-account programs, and pools. Also, additional new futures contracts continue to evolve along with futures options. Adding to the confusion, more and more attention is focused on overseas markets and their direct influence on the U.S. futures markets. It is easy to see how a trader can feel lost or overwhelmed.

Many of us are beginning to question our basic understanding of markets and the value of time-tested approaches. We have seen trading volume in the agricultural futures markets decline while volume in the financially related markets has soared. Aside from this, it is interesting to note that the switch has been from the basic, or "tangible," commodities to the intangible commodities (i.e., interest rates, stock indices, currencies). This is, no doubt, an expression of the current state of world affairs, but is, nonetheless, a reality with which all traders, veteran and novice, must contend.

Given the over-supply of information and the difficulty many traders encounter in formulating an overall trading plan, this chapter will attempt to simplify the process for you by pointing out some factors that will naturally limit your choices. Remember that the term "trading plan" does not refer to a specific system, method, or technique. It refers to an overall approach that covers virtually every aspect of trading in the market from psychology to finances. The term "trading plan" is a global term. When you are done with this chapter, you should be able to take the many different aspects of the entire book and turn them into a workable program that will, hopefully, help you accomplish many of your goals and objectives in a most efficient, enjoyable, and relatively painless fashion.

BEGIN BY LISTING YOUR LIMITATIONS

The problem most aspiring traders encounter when initiating a trading plan is that they attempt to reach for heights that are, in reality, unattainable due to limitations on the part of the trader or speculator. It is unrealistic, for example, to expect that you might continue your present occupation full-time while also attempting to successfully day trade the futures markets.

We have been told for many years that we must set our sights high if we wish to achieve great things. This may very well be true. Yet, to set goals high without building the foundation to achieve the goals guarantees frustration and failure. I would, therefore, suggest that in forming a trading plan your number one task should be to list your specific limitations, as opposed to listing your specific goals. Your goals will be directly determined and limited by the amount of input you can give toward fulfilling these goals.

HOW TO DEVELOP YOUR OWN TRADING PLAN

It's time to make a list again! And it would be wise to check it continuously. Your list should begin with a specific indication of how much time you have each day and/or week to give to the markets. You should also list precisely when you can give this time each day. Time given to the market after trading hours is distinctly different than time that can be given during the day. Among the items your list might include are the following:

1. How much time can you give the market each day (week)?

2. If you can devote time each day, what ratio of time will be given to market hours or after market hours?

3. Do you want to buy a computer?

4. What type of quote service do you want?

5. Do you need a full-commission house broker or a firm to execute trades?

6. What source of information or advisory service do you need?

7. How much of what you want to have (i.e., as above in items 3, 4, 5, and 6) is covered in the money you have allocated to trading?

8. Do you want to spend time each day watching the market, or actively trading a specific system? If so, how much time can you give?

9. Do you want to be a short-term, intermediate-term, or long-term trader?

10. Are you willing and able to take the pressure of intraday trading?

11. Are you willing to ride large losses, or are you willing to take small but more frequent losses at worst?

Many other factors, some general, some individual, should be considered as part of your list. The essence of the list is that it will limit what you can realistically attempt. This is why all trading plans must begin with your limitations.

NOW, LIST YOUR GOALS

For most traders, the goals will be financial. If so, then list them in terms of dollars, or in terms of percent return on starting capital. Once these goals have been listed, re-examine them in the light of your limitations. If you realize now that your expectations cannot become realities within the limits of your time, finances, etc., then change your goals to be in closer accord with your limitations.

You may need to go through this process several times until you have finally arrived at a workable combination. Your efforts should be directed toward setting goals that are attainable. Also, make certain that you set a practical time period within which the goals can be achieved.

THE IMPORTANCE OF BEING REALISTIC

I cannot emphasize enough the importance of being realistic in all of your dealings with the markets. There are many stories of fabulous success in the marketplace; the speculator is often tempted to believe that such success may be achieved without doing the necessary work. While it is certainly true that some individuals acquire vast fortunes in futures trading beginning with virtually nothing and within a very limited time, this is clearly the exception rather than the rule. In fact, those few traders who have amassed fortunes in brief periods of time tend to give it back to the market in a relatively short amount of time. To believe that you can achieve such results is not realistic. Your chances are about as good as those of winning one of the state lotteries. If you plan to begin trading with minimal capital and limited time input, then you are most certainly fooling yourself. While it is not my intent to discourage creative and motivating dreams, I do want to discourage virtually all traces of unrealistic thinking when it comes to success in futures trading.

If you begin (or maintain) your relationship with the market by dealing in irrational fantasies and expectations, then hopeful thinking will persist in other areas of the relationship as well. As an example, consider the wishful thinking which prompts traders to hold on to a losing position well past their stop loss point. There is also the wishful thinking that prompts traders to hold on to winning positions well past their objectives, often watching a good profit turn into a loss. This is the kind of thinking that will be stimulated by unrealistic goals. Your relationship with the market must be the single most honest relationship of your life. It requires being honest with yourself. You cannot fool the market, you can only fool yourself.

Virtually every unrealistic fantasy and action in the markets will come back to haunt you, perhaps for a long time. Hence, my severe caution is to avoid all unrealistic expectations and fantasies when you create your trading plan, and, above all, when you put it into action!

NOW DECIDE ON YOUR TRADING APPROACH

The general aspects of different trading approaches, systems, and methods are given in this book. As I have indicated, my coverage of these is very general. Once you've decided that a given approach is best suited to you within the constraints already outlined in this chapter, then acquire more information. If you're an experienced trader already employing a given approach, then take the time to reevaluate it in terms of the guidelines provided in this chapter. You may find that what you've been doing for a long time is really not for you! You may find that a totally different approach is best suited to your other needs and limitations.

The approach, system, or method you use need not be complicated, sophisticated, computer generated, or mystical. All you need is a method by which you can generate the following:

1. Entry and exit signals that have a record of accuracy in excess of 65–75 percent.

2. Specific method of entry and exit, once signals have been generated.

3. Specific objective or reversing point.

4. Specific money management of signals such as a stop loss, dollar risk amount, reversing point, etc.

5. A system that does not have periods of severe drawdown.

This last issue, drawdown, is an important one to consider in evaluating any trading system or approach.

THE IMPORTANCE OF UNDERSTANDING "DRAW-DOWN"

The hypothetical trading results of many systems are extraordinary when taken over a period of many years and when examined on the bottom line. Yet, when studied in detail, some of these systems would have required sitting through periods of severe reversals in total profit. If you had started trading such a system near a peak or just prior to a period of severe drawdown, you would have had to suffer through a period of persistent losses.

Such losses might not only cause you personal and emotional anguish, but they could easily deplete all of your risk capital, knocking you out of the game before the system recouped its losses and went on to attain major gains. Since your market entry is, in some respects, a random event, you may not be astute enough to enter at the most favorable time, thereby opening yourself to the possibility of a severe drawdown. There are a number of very cogent ways to avoid such a situation. Here are a few significant strategies for avoiding of drawdown.

1. Select systems that have shown minimal drawdown. You may have to sacrifice total performance for minimal drawdown, but it's a good tradeoff.

2. Remember that a good record of limited drawdown in the past is no guarantee of minimal drawdown in the future, but it *can* help you decide.

3. Begin trading a given system only after a period of drawdown. This may require you to wait a while before you begin trading a given system, but you will be less apt to be starting at the wrong time and you may have to sit through less of a move against you.

The last suggestion is the most important. To wait and act only after a period of drawdown would be similar to waiting for a good investment to decline in value so that you can enter on a setback, thereby reducing overall risk.

EVALUATING A TRADING RECORD

When you formulate your trading plan, select or create a system or method that best suits your needs. One of the key considerations is the performance history of the given system or method. The hypothetical (and even real-time) trading record is one of the most misunderstood things in the world of futures trading. There are so many things to remember about track records that I cannot possibly cover all of them. I can, however, give you some points I consider exceptionally important to all who are considering a given system. This holds true whether you are buying a trading system or have created your own. Please note the following vital issues!

1. Determine the maximum margin required to follow all trades and calculate this in addition to the drawdown of the system. It may take some time to figure, but it will be well

worthwhile! By knowing the absolute worst case historical scenario, you will have, at the very minimum, an idea of how bad things have gotten.

2. Take commission costs into consideration. Some hypothetical performance records do not show commission costs as losses. The cost of commissions can certainly add up. Don't forget to take these into consideration, or to recalculate the results to reflect the commissions you are paying.

3. Some performance records base profits on the purchase and sale of multiple contracts in different contract months for the same market. In other words, a system may buy or sell several different contract months in a given market at the same time. This tends to weight the profitable side of the record, often quite substantially. Be aware of this when you evaluate a record.

4. Beware of track records that have a limited history! You can prove virtually anything if your statistics are manipulated in the right way. Some trading systems show fantastic results over the last five years, yet prior to this the systems did not work well at all. Some systems work exceptionally well in bull or bear markets, but fail miserably in sideways markets. A thorough system test should include samples of performance in all markets—classic bull markets, bear markets, and sideways markets.

5. Spot check hypothetical price fills. They may assume a much better price fill than might have been possible in real time. Ideally, a system test should give the worst possible alternatives, not the best.

6. Determine how money management is used as part of the system. Is the system a reversing one, or are specific stops used with each trade? This is important since it will give you

an indication of how trades are closed out. When evaluating stops and risks, take into consideration your personal and financial abilities.

There are many other issues to consider, but I have given you highlights of those I believe deserve maximum attention.

PLAN YOUR TIME AND MAKE A SCHEDULE

Once you've made all of the major decisions, it will be time to put these decisions into practice. The best way to ruin a good trading system and good intentions is to implement them in an inconsistent or disorganized fashion. In order to utilize your time, money, and systems in the most efficient and effective way possible, you must make yourself a schedule. Your schedule should be precise. It should detail what you plan to do, how, when, and for how long. You should schedule your time and you should then follow the schedule.

It is only when you implement your plans in real time that you will be able to work out any details, limitations, or problems that you have not considered in your planning. Once you have found the schedule that works best for you, stick to it. You will know how well your schedule is working for you by your performance in the markets.

EVALUATE PROGRESS REGULARLY

Last, but certainly not least, it is important to continually evaluate the progress of your trading plan. The ultimate measure of the plan will be your performance in the markets.

However, performance itself will not tell you precisely where you have been strong or weak in your application of the rules and procedures. For this reason, you must constantly monitor your performance and implementation of the trading plan. Refer back to your list of trades frequently and study the reasons for your profits and losses. This list will, I believe, be the single most valuable source of educational feedback you will have at your disposal. If you keep it up to date and if you are totally honest in your record keeping, then you will benefit greatly.

SUMMARY

This chapter gave specific suggestions regarding the formulation of a trading plan. Emphasis was placed upon analysis of performance records, organization, and accurate record-keeping.

Chapter

18

Managing Risk: Second Key to Success

Futures trading can be characterized as a highly unstructured environment. Unlike other social activities, such as sports or business, trading futures does not have a defined beginning and end. In addition, futures trading does not have a prescribed set of rules to guide your behavior. It is this open-ended and unstructured setting that makes trading a challenging and risky endeavor. Without defined structure, the market environment provides the potential for unlimited opportunity as well as unlimited risk.

If you think of the futures market as a wide open field with unlimited possibilities, you may begin to see the need for creating your own personal rules to guide your behavior. You need to define the structure and this requires that you define the risk you are willing to assume. A good risk management program, if followed properly, will help you to define risk and develop the rules to manage the risk.

One of the inherent aversions to developing a risk management program is the fear of responsibility. Most traders want the excitement and the chance to capitalize on the markets without applying the rigorous steps to minimize their risk. To become a successful trader, you must be willing to assume responsibility. To be responsible requires a commitment to manage your risk coupled with a willingness to learn from your losses.

What I propose to do in this chapter is to give you some guidelines by which you can learn the necessary distinctions for managing risk.

Since most trades in the futures markets are closed out as losses, we must use losses as a learning tool. Though this is not the ideal situation, the market is not a patient or reliable teacher. In fact, the market is an inconsistent teacher. Sometimes the market will reward you for doing the wrong thing and sometimes it will punish you for doing the right thing. As you can easily see, the marketplace is a difficult and unpredictable environment in which to learn. We must, therefore, pay attention to what we can learn from the market. We must make the most of the market feedback we get. This feedback, the raw material of our learning, consists primarily of losses, but to some extent, of profits as well.

WHEN YOU MAKE A TRADE; WHEN YOU CLOSE OUT A TRADE

The first important bit of advice I can give regarding losses and profits is to keep a detailed record of all trades. I suggest you keep the following information on every single trade.

1. **Entry and Exit Date, Entry and Exit Prices**
    This is, of course, standard procedure.

2. **Reason for Making the Trade**
    This is a very important aspect of the record-keeping approach. By forcing yourself to list the reason(s) for each and every trade, you will be forced to stick to your trading system rules. You will avoid the temptation of making trades

on whims, tips, or inside information. You'll avoid the temp-tation to jump into and out of trades based on factors which are not related to your trading system or method. In other words, this will force you to think before you act. This prac-tice will help reduce impulsive trades that, in the long run, are losing trades.

By adding this simple requirement to your record-keeping system you will help avoid mistakes. In addition, you will have a permanent record of why each trade was made. If you entered the trade within the parameters of your system or method and ended up taking a loss, you'll be able to go back over the record in order to evaluate your decision. Per-haps you made a mistake in understanding your indicators or signals. Having clear records are always more reliable than memory.

3. **Reason for Closing out Position**
   This is just as important as point 2. This will help you pin-point the exact reasoning you employed in closing out a trade. Many traders can enter a trade for the right reasons, but they go astray when it comes to closing out. They tend to become emotional once in a trade. Emotion can cause them to either stay too long, riding a loss, or to get out too soon, taking a profit that might have been much larger in the long run. Therefore, make certain you keep a thorough record of why trades were closed out.

4. **Reason for Profit or Loss**
   By studying or analyzing the reasons for your profits or losses (as indicated by items 2 and 3), you will be able to analyze what you are doing right and what you are doing wrong. Generally, you will see that the reasons for your losses tend to cluster around the same types of errors. These will, most often, be emotional as opposed to technical. With most trading systems you'll take as many as 6-8 losses out of

10 trades due to the nature of trading systems. However, if you're taking 8 or more losses out of 10 trades, and if the reasons are not directly due to the system error rate itself, then you will know very quickly by examining your record.

STUDY THE RECORD REGULARLY AND FREQUENTLY

Once you have mastered the record-keeping aspect, you will need to study the record regularly. If you're an active trader, then study the record at the end of every trading day and review your learning the next morning before the markets open. If you are not an active trader, then once weekly will be sufficient.

I strongly urge you to understand each and every loss and not to trade again until you do. If you study the record and force yourself to learn from it, then your losses will truly help you grow. Failure to employ losses in the fashion I have outlined means that you are not using your tuition wisely.

Furthermore, by studying your losses, you will be able to determine very quickly what has gone wrong. You can decide if errors were trader errors, system errors, broker errors, etc. You will know very quickly if your trading system is at fault. If this is clearly the case, then you will be able to change systems. If, on the other hand, you find that you are at fault, you will be able to take the action required to make the changes.

PROFITS CAN HELP YOU LEARN

In your quest for reasons and explanations and in your efforts to learn, don't overlook the importance of learning from profits, as well. A profit will let you know when you've done something correctly, but don't be fooled into thinking that profits can only come from correct action. At times, the market will generate a profit whether or not you acted correctly. The market is not entirely consistent. If the market was a bastion of consistency, then there would be no reason for writing this book.

Be very careful about profits that come after a behavior that was not appropriate. In other words, assume you did something incorrect, but that you were rewarded with a profit. This is a potentially dangerous situation since you may be setting yourself up for the beginning of bad trading habits. The profit will reward you for doing something that was not consistent with your system or with effective trading behavior.

If you find that your application of trading rules and principles is resulting in profits most of the time, then you are on the right track and you should stay on it!

HOW MUCH CAPITAL SHOULD YOU RISK?

As I mentioned near the beginning of the book, the more capital you have to start trading, the greater potential you have for surviving the markets. I stressed that if your initial margin on a position is $2,500, then you should have a minimum of $12,500 to trade with. This 10 percent rule can also be applied to the amount you are willing to risk on each trade. The maximum to risk on any one trade is 10 percent, but you may feel more comfortable risking less. Anything more than 10 percent will affect your ability to survive even a small string of losses.

USING STOP-LOSS ORDERS

It is often said that getting into the market is easy; it's getting out that's tough. One key management rule you can use to manage risk is to place stop-loss orders after you initiate a position. It is easy to think about what you are willing to risk before you get into a trade, but it is another story once you are in the market. Having a stop-loss order in place will automatically limit your downside. I should add that keeping a stop-loss order will limit your risk. Oftentimes traders will place the stop-loss order in the market, only to cancel when the market gets close to the order. This is a dangerous habit to develop and can lead to big losses. Getting into the practice of using stop-loss orders will protect your equity and keep you disciplined.

DON'T OVERTRADE

One of the pitfalls that even experienced traders fall into is overtrading. The tendency to get caught up in the emotion of the market, especially after a string of winning trades, can make it tempting to trade larger than you should. With the relatively low margin requirements, traders can get leverage crazy and a "the bigger the better" mentality starts to set in. This has been the demise of many traders and should not be taken lightly. Whatever you do, remember that consistency in keeping risk management rules is of utmost importance. When you forget this simple fact, your emotions take over and losses will begin to accumulate. Plan your trade, trade your plan, and stick with your rules!

LEARN TO STAND ASIDE WHEN YOU'RE CONFUSED

Many traders feel they must be in the markets at all times. Nothing could be more inaccurate. If you are confused or uncertain, remove yourself from the game and observe for awhile. Even if you have been consistent with your application of the trading rules and have done your best to learn from your losses, stand aside if things feel uncertain.

The newcomer cannot trade without understanding the ups and downs of trading, and knowing when he or she has reached the limit.

DON'T TAKE LOSSES PERSONALLY

There is no doubt that losses are painful. Every loss hurts, but it can hurt more if your attitude toward losses is a negative one. If you look upon each loss as an opportunity to learn, and if you look upon your initial risk capital as tuition, expecting to lose most of it, your attitude toward losses will be a positive one.

If you do not take each loss as a personal defeat, then you will not allow losses to negatively affect your behavior in the market. Your approach to futures trading should be similar to the approach of any individual entering a new business. You must take about a year to learn the business, and you must not expect your first year to be a winning one.

Futures trading appears to take longer to learn any other business I know. As a matter of fact, the learning process in futures trading never stops. There are always lessons to learn. Hopefully, with the passage of time, the losses will become less frequent and the lessons will not have to be learned over and over again. But, all of this can only be achieved if you have the proper attitude toward losses. Failure to do so will likely inhibit the learning process.

COMPETITION

It has been said that competition is a healthy thing. While this may be true for the professional athlete, it is not necessarily true for the futures trader. In sports, you know who it is that you are competing against. In the futures market, however, you do not know your foe. If you envision your rival to be the entire market, then you have set yourself an impossible task, since you will never defeat the entire market.

Who, then, should your competitor be? I maintain that you must always compete with yourself. Do not look at what other traders have done. Do not attempt to out do their success. Don't set your standards so terribly high that you will never be able to achieve them. The market holds a vast treasure with sufficient wealth for many traders. Naturally, not all traders can be winners. Losers must feed the pot, but the rational futures trader will seek to dip into the pot for only a small portion of its immense wealth.

You must always be your own chief rival. Compete with your own results. Try to better your own record. There will always be someone who claims to be doing better than you are. This should be of no consequence to you.

The ego of a trader is very important. There are literally hundreds of potentially ego-deflating experiences the market can unleash upon the trader. But the trader will only be vulnerable if he or she opens the door to such experiences. The ego of a trader is fragile. Many things can affect it. The greatest of these is losses. As you know, many losses are unnecessary. If the reasons for losses are known and eliminated, then the ego will be protected and the many errors a trader can make due to emotional response of ego involvement will be eliminated as well.

TAKE AN ASSESSMENT OF YOUR LOSSES— IT'S NOT TOO LATE!

Many of us feel we are not achieving our true potential in the markets. We know we are taking unnecessary losses. We know we are not as disciplined as we should be. We know we can do something to improve but we don't know what. The best thing to do is to begin learning from losses immediately. Begin the record-keeping approach I've described. If you're a newcomer to futures or a veteran trader, get started on the right path immediately. It's not too late!

SUMMARY

Many traders do not know how to manage risk. This chapter gave specific ways to manage risk and to preserve capital. Knowing the amount to risk on each trade, utilizing orders to manage risk exposure, and learning from your profits and losses were some of the concepts covered.

Chapter

19

What You Need to Know about Computers

With the tremendous growth and popularity of home computer systems in recent years, it is almost a heresy to say that very few individuals actually need computers. While it is true that personal computer systems have made many things easier for the businessperson, I suspect that their use, with a few specific exceptions, has been generally overrated.

Today, for example, there are many novice traders who feel that they cannot be successful in futures trading without a computer quote system and/or a computer trading system. I'm from the old school. I emphatically insist that success is not computer-dependent in today's futures markets. It is perfectly possible for virtually any aspiring futures trader to be successful without a computer, without a "quote system," and without a computerized trading system.

The public relations and advertising jobs unleashed upon the public worldwide have apparently had their desired effect in attracting many new followers to the fold. My long-standing point of view is that the decision to buy a computer for futures trading should receive considerable deliberation before a commitment is made. Not only are computers expensive, but their maintenance is not *gratis*. The overall expense of purchasing, maintaining, and operating a computer may be prohibitive to the new futures trader.

These days, it seems more and more that the decision is not whether one should get a computer trading system, but rather which system will do the job the best. Although my advice to a good majority of futures traders is that they don't really need a computer system or a computerized trading method, I know that my words will fall on deaf ears. If you have already set your mind on buying a computer, then at the very least follow some guidelines in making your decision.

I will cover the subject in as simple terms as possible, since I know that computer jargon can be quite difficult to follow. It should also be remembered with the rapid changes occurring almost daily in the field of computer technology, any specific comments I could make about a particular system or systems would certainly be out of date by the time you have purchased and read this book. Therefore, my comments will be generic, and hopefully in this way they will have a longer shelf life.

DO YOU REALLY NEED A COMPUTER?

Assuming you have not already made your decision about purchasing a computer system, I suggest you take a number of points into consideration before you reach your decision. If you have already made your decision, but have not purchased a system, consider these points as well, since they may affect your final selections.

1. **What Will the System Do for You?**
    If your futures trading system is highly complex and requires considerable mathematical manipulation on a frequent basis, then you have no choice but to purchase a computer. In addition, if research of futures systems and methods is what you intend to do, then the computer will be

absolutely necessary. In each case, remember that an additional and significant cost of the system will be the data and the programming.

You may do the programming yourself, or you may purchase some prepackaged software. The cost of data is still something to consider when determining your total expense. You must also remember that continuous data updates will be required if you plan to use the system in real time and/or if you plan to update your research regularly.

Unless these two significant computer applications are your goals, the odds are that what you wish to accomplish can probably be done with a sophisticated hand-held calculator, or with a very small microcomputer at significantly lower cost than a full-fledged personal computer system.

In order to fully determine your need for a computer, you should also attempt to evaluate your future needs based on the requirements of the system or systems you plan to use. A good rule of thumb is to determine how long it takes you to generate your trading signals each day. Many systems can be updated manually in a matter of minutes every day, whereas others may require several hours to produce trading signals. Certainly, several hours of calculations every day can be quite tedious, and a computer would clearly prove cost-effective in such a case.

Since I recommend that novices use only simple trading systems requiring minimal time input and expense, a conservative approach to an otherwise high-risk venture is usually a sensible balance. Assuming that you have decided to purchase a computer system after considering the expense, usefulness, maintenance costs, programming cost, and data costs, you may now read on to some of the other general areas of importance. If you have decided not to purchase a computer system, you can skip the balance of this chapter.

2. **What Will You Need in a System?**
    The weak link in any computer system is not necessarily the
    computer memory, but rather the storage and printer capa-
    bilities. This is so because the printer is normally the slowest
    peripheral device and the storage device(s) the most used. If
    you are like most futures traders, you will want to purchase
    a system that will provide good graphics in hard copy form
    (i.e., on paper off the printer) so that you may study charts,
    chart patterns, and price relationships. You will also want to
    study large amounts of data.

    Even if chart patterns are not what you wish to analyze, you
    will need your printer for getting hard-copy results of any
    research programs you plan to run on your data. Therefore,
    I would consider the printer one of the most important links
    in the chain, and certainly the most vulnerable one.

    When buying a system, attempt to get a printer of reason-
    ably high speed and very high resolution. The storage de-
    vice(s) is (are) also important. Storage is discussed below.

3. **Storage.**
    One of the most important features of any computer system
    is the amount of data it will store on disk. With more and
    more historical data added to the base with each passing
    day, as well as with the growing trend for intraday data
    analysis, the more storage you can get, the better off you will
    be in terms of saved labor. There are many different types of
    storage systems available. These range from tape storage to
    floppy disk to hard disk. Ideally, hard disk storage of ap-
    proximately 30 megabytes should be sufficient to keep on
    file data for virtually every futures contract on a daily basis
    for the last 15 years. Having such storage capabilities will
    permit you to analyze virtually any program on every mar-
    ket in your database without having to change disks. This
    will permit you to be away from your computer system
    doing other productive work while the system is busy

crunching numbers. I would suggest that if additional money is going to be spent, it should be spent on storage as opposed to memory.

If computer programs are efficiently written in an assembler language or in some other noninterpretive computer instruction, then smaller memory will be sufficient, with larger storage being more important. Large storage is an absolute necessity for those wishing to perform complex, historical analyses or intraday studies.

4. **CPU (Mainframe)**.
The CPU (central processing unit) is the heart of the system hardware. Memory size is an important consideration when researching price patterns. Although many computer users get carried away with large computer memory, efficient programming can circumvent the need for large memory. With the cost of add-on memory becoming lower all the time, I suggest that you consider the cost to memory ratio in making your final decision. If you can add considerably more memory at reasonably low cost then, by all means, do so. But remember that storage is more important than memory.

5. **Compatibility**.
Many good computer systems on today's market can be had at very low prices, but some are not essentially compatible with the software or data stream provided by the popular computer services. The trend has been for most data to be written specifically for use with the most popular software and the most popular computer systems. In view of these limitations, your choices of hardware will probably be very limited since the cost of producing new software to accommodate an off-brand computer system may be prohibitive.

Some individuals may wish to use a specific computerized trading system produced by a given software firm. In such cases, the trader will be constrained by the limitations of the hardware system for which the software was originally written.

The issue of compatibility is becoming more important every day. While there have been many upstart software firms and "clone" hardware systems, the battle has slowly but surely been won by a few of the larger hardware firms and only several of the manufacturers of clone-type systems have survived.

Today, much good research and trading systems software is written for only two or three specific hardware systems. Though this is a fairly typical result of competition, it does, unfortunately, limit the choices of hardware available to you.

REINVENT THE WHEEL?

The almost continuous stream of futures trading software that now dominates the marketplace has turned from a slow trickle into a virtual waterfall of programs. Competition is becoming greater every day, and rarely a day passes without a new program or system being presented to the public for sale or lease. The response of the public has been quite positive and futures software sales have been booming.

In some cases, there may be so many users of a particular system that this could, to a certain extent, affect its operations. However, the large number of alternatives and competitive systems on today's market makes the likelihood of too many traders following any one particular system rather small. This speaks favorably about the possibility of profiting from one of the commercially available systems.

The independent trader will probably want to avoid most commercially available trading systems in favor of developing his or her own trading approach using concepts and techniques he or she has developed. This is, of course, the ideal application of computer systems and the results may justify the entire cost of the system many times over.

You should also know that if you are interested in trading software development, there are some utility programs available that may considerably cut down on your work. Specifically, you can purchase a pre-written program that will allow you to input various parameters for test purposes. You may then generate hypothetical trading results more quickly and specifically without having to go through all of the programming work from start to finish. With the passage of time, I am certain many more programs will be available that ultimately may eliminate most of the individual research required in software development.

Although the decision to develop or use pre-written software is certainly an individual one, the rapid changes and accelerating progress in futures trading software research make it worth your while to consider a pre-written program as opposed to developing your own systems. Unfortunately, the purchase of a pre-written program eliminates much of the challenge of this game. Yet, the challenge of making profits is still the greatest one indeed! Consider also the possibility of modifying existing software to more closely suit your needs or, perhaps, to vastly improve its performance.

COMPUTERIZED QUOTE SYSTEMS

The days of the large mechanical quote board that clicked and ticked away in the broker's office are almost history. The familiar sound of rapidly changing prices has been replaced by the complete silence of the green screen and the occasional beeping of a computer reminding its master that something of importance has occurred. The hand-drawn chart has been replaced by the familiar dot matrix of the computer printer, and the good, old fashioned colored lines and colored pencils are now also victims of progress.

Yet, in spite of our wonderful technology, there are still many significant differences between quote systems. Virtually no barrier has been a significant one if cost is no object. The single best way to determine the type of quotation system best suited for your purposes is to test drive them. If you cannot arrange for a no-cost trial period, then attempt to visit a broker or friend who has a system and use it for a while to see how you relate to it. Different systems have different strengths and weaknesses. Certainly you would hate to purchase a system and be stuck with it if it is not ideally suited to the precise applications you require.

SUMMARY

The advent of home computer systems has broadened the scope of futures traders. We can now analyze massive amounts of data in a matter of minutes. The net effect, however, has now been minimized since the advantage is now available to virtually all traders whether through their own computer systems or via the purchase of research performed by various services.

The computer trading revolution may, however, be illusory. Many traders, particularly novices, are convinced that they cannot attain success in futures without a computer. This chapter debunked the computer dependency myth. It provided some specific guidelines upon which to evaluate computer systems. I emphasized the point that a computer is not necessary for success. I outlined some reasons for buying or not buying a computer system.

Part

5

Computers, Trading Systems, and You

Chapter

20

Computerized Trading Systems— Tricks With Statistics or Reality?

Computer testing of mechanical trading systems has grown considerably since the early 1980s. Traders may easily verify the claims of system developers. The trading public need not be victimized by fallacious assertions regarding trading systems. While the software to test systems is readily available, it is necessary to know the essential ingredients which comprise a successful test. Many traders today underestimate the ability of some promoters to manipulate statistics. Systems developers can "massage" statistics in order to show favorable results. Individual traders tend to deceive themselves in testing their own systems. Having high expectations and wishful thinking, they too fall prey to the fallacy of confusing past performance with future results.

In order to determine the validity of any system, it is crucial to remember that simply reporting highly favorable results does not guarantee success with that system in real-time trading. The basic assumption, "the better it worked in the past, the better it will work in the future," has been one of the more costly beliefs to traders. Unfortunately, a misguided objective of many testing systems is to develop trading strategies that extract the greatest possible profit from historical data. Such optimum systems are not designed to portray the worst case scenarios, but rather, are developed to demonstrate optimum past performance. This is not only naive, but potentially dangerous.

WHY TEST A TRADING SYSTEM?

Why is it necessary to test a system? If testing any system only gives you hypothetical results with no guaranteed success in real-time trading, why bother? Although you will never really know for certain if a system will work in the future (in real time with real money) proper testing methods can allow you to learn the strong and weak aspects of your system.

Traders have their different reasons for testing systems. Some test a system to "go through the motions," failing to take seriously the results. All too often, they disregard the results or rationalize poor results. They mistakenly believe that they can turn a mediocre system into a winner by managing the trades differently or by practicing different money management rules. Other traders develop systems in order to market them to the public. Their objective is to optimize the system in order to reflect best case performance. In effect, the "ultimate product" that they are trying to sell is a contrived system, curve fitted to an extreme degree. As attractive as they may seem, the odds of such systems working in real-time trading are slim indeed. Any statistician acquainted with the law of diminishing returns understands that the more variables and rules you add to a system, the less reliable the outcome will be.

The serious trader who tests systems with the rigor and discipline needed for success in the futures markets must have specific goals. Their reasons for testing systems are as follows:

1. To determine whether a hypothetical construct is valid in historical testing. How would the idea have performed in the past?

2. To learn the assets and the liabilities of the system.

3. To identify how potentially different timing indicators combine with one another to produce a potentially effective trading system.

4. To examine the relationship of risk and reward variables (i.e., entry and exit methods using stops, position size, etc.) which would have produced the best overall performance with the smallest drawdown (to be explained more fully later).

Since the time and expense of real-time testing a new trading system are considerable, it follows that computer testing is the most efficient method for determining how a system would have performed in the past. The main purpose of testing systems is to learn what might work best in the future based on what has worked in the past. Do not, however, expect to find a 100 percent correlation between the past and the future. Nothing is definite in futures. There are various important aspects which must be considered when you test any trading system. These should include the following:

1. **Number of Years Analyzed.**
    It would seem logical to assume that the further back you test the system, the better the results will be. In fact, the opposite is true. Many trading systems and indicators do not withstand the test of time. The further back you test, the less effective most systems will be. A standard test of ten years is preferred by many system developers since it presents their

systems best. The more important variable in testing systems is the number of trades rather than the number of years analyzed.

2. **Number of Trades Analyzed.**
    Analyzing data over the course of many years is not necessary if you have a large sample size of trades. I feel that at least 100 trades is required to produce statistically significant results, provided your system will generate this number of trades in back testing. It is better to err on the side of more rather than less data. It would not be wise to select a model based on just a few trades that occurred during a circumscribed period of time. Such a system would not work in market conditions distinctly different than those tested.

3. **Maximum Drawdown.**
    A very important, but overlooked statistic is percent equity drawdown. A system that generates a very high annualized percent return over a period of five years will be difficult to follow if it has drawdowns of 50 percent several times during that five-year period. It would take guts and a highly capitalized account to handle the equity swings. In my experience, a smooth equity curve is much more desirable.

    This curve is important as it illustrates how practical your trading system will be with real money. It seems that most systems that give the largest net profits have the largest drawdowns. Look at a large drawdown coupled with a string of losses and it is easy to see why most people may prematurely abandon a potentially good trading system. People are generally more interested in trading systems that reflect steady growth and small drawdowns, rather than the "home-runs" showing big short-term gains with large drawdowns.

4. **Maximum Successive Losses.**
    While these can be painful, maximum consecutive losers can be useful. It gives you an idea of how much emotional pain

you may have to endure while trading your system. There are few traders who are willing to stick with their system after three or four consecutive losers. Oftentimes, they abandon a potentially good system. A forecast of this number can help prepare a trader for a worst case scenario and prevent panic when it actually happens.

5. **Largest Single Losing Trade.**
This is especially important if it exceeds your normal risk-control measure. There may a problem or contingency you have overlooked. A natural tendency of traders is to overlook the biggest losing trades and to psychologically eliminate them. You will often see practices of curve fitting to compensate for the loss, which is deceptive, misleading, and potentially costly. If you pay attention to the single losing trade, you can learn where to adjust the initial stop loss and manage the overall system with efficiency. You should also use this information to question why the largest single losing trade was bigger than the stop loss you had selected. The whole idea of testing a system is to avoid surprises that can negate your whole system.

6. **Largest Single Winning Trade.**
In some ways the largest winning trade is more important to pay attention to since it can skew the net profit in an unreasonable way. It might be best to eliminate the largest winning trade in each commodity and then reevaluate the net results. As I mentioned earlier, the goal is toward consistency. An extremely large winning trade can misconstrue the overall results of the system's performance.

7. **Percentage of Winning Trades.**
This statistic is not as important as you may think and can often be misleading. For example, most successful traders have 30 percent to 45 percent winners. Systems which reflect 80 percent accuracy can be bad systems. When you actually do some testing, you will see that it is difficult to get much

over 55 percent winners in a system. It is also significant to be aware of the effect stops have on winning percentages.

8. Do not trust any testing results that don't include a liberal allowance for slippage and commissions. They can make a very big difference in your overall results. There are many trading systems that will make small steady profits when tested without slippage and commissions, then turn into steady losers when transaction costs are factored in. You must pay particular attention to the transaction costs when the system operates on short-term trades or day-trading. The more often trades are generated, the more critical transaction costs become. Everyone has favorite numbers to factor in as transaction costs. I like to use $75 for slippage and $50 for commission per round turn for a total of $125 per trade. This number may seem high, but I prefer to err on the conservative side and avoid unpleasant surprises. While you may initially want to exclude the transaction costs to simplify the operation, make sure they are included before you look at potential bottom-line results. Commission costs and slippage add up and can make an incredible difference in your testing results.

9. **Ratio of Average Win to Average Loss.**
   There is a tendency among traders to assume that you must have a proportionately high number of winners to losers in a system. Obviously, the ratio should be well over 1-to-1 (break-even). Ideally we would all like to have a ratio of 3-to-1 or 4-to-1 winners to losers, but given a decent percentage of winners, a 2-to-1 ratio will produce plenty of profit.

SUMMARY

Computer testing of mechanical trading systems has grown in the last ten years. The ability to verify claims of systems developers has increased due to the development of these testing systems. Today, however, systems developers use statistic manipulation to show optimum performance of a system. Oftentimes this is a distortion and does not adequately reflect how a system will perform in real time. The trader needs to be aware that systems developers "massage" statistics to market their trading programs. Learning to evaluate the validity of testing systems is covered in this chapter. There are different reasons for testing systems. I listed the reasons a serious trader tests a system and the important criteria necessary for evaluating a testing system. With so many traders using computers to design and test trading systems, it is important to examine the testing process itself and to identify the common mistakes that can affect your bottom line. It is important to remember that testing is the means to an end, not an end in itself and in realizing this you will become aware that reporting highly favorable results does not in any way guarantee success in the future. The goal of testing is to learn the good and the bad about your system and to begin to know what to expect in the future. A good trading system will reflect slow, steady growth and consistent performance.

Chapter

21

Artificial Intelligence and Neural Networks: Myth or Messiah?

The application of neural network technology to computerized futures trading systems has become very popular. Neural networks differ from other standardized programs in that they have "thinking" ability. They also have adaptable processing capabilities that enable a system to recognize price patterns to a degree which has heretofore been impossible. For trading purposes, the ability of neural networks to learn from trial and error may prove to be one of the most significant advances ever in trading systems.

With the rapid progress in neural network technology it is easy to fall into the trap of thinking that they may be the "perfect" systems. While neural networks do offer efficient ways to perceive market opportunities, the role of risk management and trader discipline cannot be ignored. As I have already pointed out, and cannot emphasize enough, emotions gone astray will continue to limit the possibility of all trading systems, no matter how promising their back-tested results may be.

ARTIFICIAL INTELLIGENCE

Neural network programs are distinctly different from conventional software applications. And they do not fit within the realm of traditional artificial intelligence (AI). Historically, the approach to designing computerized systems has been based on rules and symbols. While symbol processing enables computers to perform thinking tasks such as math and logic problems faster and more accurately than our brains can, they are limited in their ability to generate new thinking. Traditionally, computers are given a list of instructions to follow and therefore are unable to create new patterns which fall outside of the limits of predetermined programs.

Until recently, computer systems have been based on simulations of human decision-making processes. Artificial intelligence, however, has been developed by computer scientists who view the working of the human mind as a metaphor by which to explain the operation of the computer. This explanation has been both a help as well as a hindrance. Unfortunately, it has been assumed that the mind is best understood in its own terms: as a collection of ideas and arguments.

While this rule-based model of the mind has been appealing to AI researchers and psychologists, it has been limiting in its ability to explain common sense-type thinking and generative thinking. Recently, however, researchers have been replacing the rule-driven description of our thinking processes, with a new model that attempts to duplicate the circuitry of the brain. The shift toward considering the complex interaction of the brain's billions of neurons is now being reflected in the structure of neural networks.

CHARACTERISTICS OF NEURAL NETWORKS

Neural networks differ from AI and standard programming practices in a number of significant ways. Neural nets are built with components modeled after the neuron and grouped in interconnected nets.

Unlike digital computers, neural nets don't have a "central processor" that operates on a few bits of data at a time. Instead, like our brains, the neurons act on data all at once, bringing the entire system to bear on a problem. Also, similar to our brains, memories in a neural net are spread throughout the network; they are not isolated in a separate memory bank.

Neural nets process information differently than do traditional programs. Each neuron evaluates signals from other neuron-like components and then "decides" on the basis of the answer as to whether it should send out a signal of its own.

Furthermore, standard programming practices rely on a list of instructions. A neural network, however, is "taught" through a series of examples. After being exposed to specific patterns as examples, the machine eventually "learns" to make the judgments on its own, even on patterns it has not seen before. This is, of course, the theory which is yet to be developed into practice.

Neural networks have the ability to produce answers quickly due to their more flexible style of information processing. Like our brains, neural nets can draw inferences, form categories, and make associations. In his book, *Neural Network Design and the Complexity of Learning,* J. Stephen Judd comments on the thinking process of neural networks:

> ". . . aside from generalizing, neural networks seem to extrapolate their learned knowledge to other parts of their domain that they have not had access to thereby performing something of great value beyond mere storage."[1]

NEURAL NETWORKS AND TRADING

The risks, complexity, and volatile nature of futures markets require sophisticated methods of viewing and interpreting market data. Neural networks can be helpful in evaluating technical indicators

---

1   Judd, J. Stephen. *Neural Network Design and the Complexity of Learning,* MIT Press, 1990, p. 187.

through their ability to recognize patterns. Neural networks also appear to improve their performance with experience.

While neural networks hold great promise for futures and equity traders, caution is advised. There is no ultimate tool for winning the trading game. At times any technology, no matter how promising, may fail. At times the technology is poorly managed. Some traders, although encouraged by the potential of a sophisticated neural network program, discipline themselves to take orders from a machine, and eventually sabotage the program. The emotional limitations of traders must never be underestimated. It can undo all constructive inputs in short order.

Neural networks ability to match patterns, form generalizations, merge new situations into old, mirror existing structures, and find the best fit among many scenarios are all promising attributes. Coupled with sound trading rules and disciplined risk management, neural networks can provide traders with great potential for success. I stress, however, that the potential cannot be fulfilled unless accompanied by an effective program of risk management and trading discipline.

Chapter

22

Summing It All Up

What I have attempted to achieve in this book is bound to meet with praise and prejudice. Those who understand that the game of futures trading is not what it appears to be on the surface, but rather a test of behavior, discipline, emotion, and skill, will truly appreciate the lessons this book has conveyed. To those who believe that to understand futures and to trade them successfully you need only acquire or develop a good system, this book will have been of no help. Those who have experienced the frustration of having a potentially successful trading system, yet not showing tangible benefits from its application, may have found some important answers within these pages.

Ultimately, the true test of your learning and my teaching will be your ability to put the concepts and suggestions I have provided into successful action. For those who have already learned and internalized the directions and suggestions made in this book, the review will hopefully have proven valuable. Sometimes, as you know, it is necessary to learn and relearn lessons many times until they are truly learned. A lesson that must be relearned has not been learned.

Those who are, by their own lifestyle and perception of reality fixed in the mistaken belief that futures trading is based entirely upon knowing the facts will have learned otherwise in this book. Those who know that the facts of futures trading are of secondary importance to the issues of self-control, discipline, self-confidence, and consistency will have found their beliefs and values strongly confirmed.

We are always tempted to search for better answers, better systems, better methods, and better techniques. This search is the motivating force that drives the consumer to buy literally millions of dollars worth of computer hardware, software, charts, books, tapes, trading systems, and seminars every year. In their search for the external, most futures traders persistently ignore the value and importance of the internal. As you can tell by now, the emphasis of this book has been on the internal. Virtually everything I've said in the preceding chapters can be summarized by the following quotation from Lao Tsu:

> "There is no need to run outside For better seeing, Nor to peer from a window. Rather abide at the center of your being; For the more you leave it, the less you learn. Search your heart and see if he is wise who takes each turn: The way to do is to be."[1]

In closing, my original temptation was to tell you that, "My task has ended and yours just begun." However, this is not the case. My life and time in futures trading have made me understand that no matter what my goals happen to be, I am always at the beginning of my task. Each challenge unfolds a task of greater importance and another step on the road to market mastery.

---

1   Bynner, W., *The Way of Life According to Lao Tzu*, Capricorn 1944.

Index

About the Publisher

PROBUS PUBLISHING COMPANY

Probus Publishing Company fills the informational needs of today's business professional by publishing authoritative, quality books on timely and relevant topics, including:

- Investing
- Futures/Options Trading
- Banking
- Finance
- Marketing and Sales
- Manufacturing and Project Management
- Personal Finance, Real Estate, Insurance and Estate Planning
- Entrepreneurship
- Management

Probus books are available at quantity discounts when purchased for business, educational or sales promotional use. For more information, please call the Director, Corporate/Institutional Sales at 1-800-PROBUS-1, or write:

Director, Corporate/Institutional Sales
Probus Publishing Company
1925 N. Clybourn Avenue
Chicago, Illinois 60614
FAX (312) 868-6250

Additional Titles by
Jake Bernstein Available from Probus Publishing

*Analysis & Forecasting of Long-Term Trends in the Cash and Futures
Market*

*Timing Signals in the Futures Market: The Trader's Guide to Buy/Sell
Indicators*

*Why Traders Lose, How Traders Win: Timing Futures Trades with Daily
Market Sentiment*

Forthcoming Titles

*Short-Term Futures Trading: Systems, Strategies, & Techniques for the
Day-Trader.* Anticipated Publication Date: November 1992.